Letters from
the Heart

Father Michael Seed s.a.
with Noel Botham

BLAKE

Published by Blake Publishing Ltd,
3 Bramber Court, 2 Bramber Road,
London W14 9PB, England

First published in the UK, 2000

ISBN 1 85782 461 X

British Library Cataloguing-in-Publication data:
A catalogue record for this book is available from the British Library.

Designed by GDAdesign

Printed in Great Britain by
Creative Print and Design (Wales), Ebbw Vale, Gwent

1 3 5 7 9 10 8 6 4 2

Addresses have been edited in the interests of security.

With thanks to Piers Morgan at *The Mirror* and to *The Universe* for the use of photographs.
Thanks also to Sally Soames for the photograph of Father Michael Seed and to St Paul's
Publishing for permission to use some letters from the original edition.
Every attempt has been made to contact the the photograph copyright holders, but
some proved uncontactable. We would be grateful if those concerned could contact us.

Thoughts on heaven from the rich, the

Dedication

*Dedicated to the life and memory
of Mother Teresa of Calcutta and
Cardinal Basil Hume.*

is, the poor, the needy and the notorious

Contents

Introduction

Acknowledgements

Heaven...

And Love

On Earth

And Sacrifice

Thoughts on heaven from the rich, the

In Heaven

And Light

And Life

And Faith

s, the poor, the needy and the notorious

Death and Dying

And Peace

Joy and Hope

And Praise

And Friends and Family

Thoughts on heaven from the rich, the

Thoughts on heaven from the rich, the

Introduction

'My idea of heaven' said the Victorian cleric Sydney Smith 'is eating *pâté de foie gras* to the sound of trumpets.' To others this might easily be a description of hell. No two people's ideas of heaven are ever exactly alike. To one person it is a chocolate factory, to others a place where bread always lands butter–side up.

I discovered this great variety of views when I was approached to write a book on heaven. At first I was perplexed. What words could I use? How would I even start to express it? I was tempted to tell the publishers that I could not produce such a book, but began to reconsider when friends and colleagues, to whom I had mentioned the invitation, started to give their thoughts on what heaven meant to them. Some were moving, some thought provoking, and a few were quite outrageously funny.

It prompted me to write to other people around the world, and ask them for their views on heaven. The answers came flooding back from children, the old, the famous, the rich and poor, the religious and the non-believers.

By the summer I had finished editing the letters, and it was one of them, a transcript of a conversation in which an eight-year-old believed that heaven is a place where dogs don't bite, that inspired the title of that first book: *I Will See You In Heaven Where Animals Don't Bite*.

The first heaven book was produced by a church-related publisher, and was available from mainly religious outlets, which meant it reached a very limited audience. I was therefore delighted when, in 1998, I was encouraged by the author Noel Botham and publisher John Blake, to seek fresh contributions for a new version of the book which would be accessible to everyone and which would form a small part of the Millennium celebrations.

I am deeply indebted to all those people who so kindly gave their time to reflect on the question: What is heaven to you? Faced with this, most of them probably suffered a mental block. That was my first reaction too. But when they really thought about it, most felt able to respond.

Their responses are remarkably different. Some are complicated, others simple. Some wry, others profound. The heaven that springs from these pages is a warm, funny, unusual and welcoming place. There is space for everyone: from the richest to the poorest, highest to the lowest, saint to the sinner.

Sometimes we are inclined to think that heaven is only for special people: just for saints in stained glass windows. But this wasn't the heaven of Jesus Christ. He said 'In my father's house there are many rooms.' This remark was scandalous then and continues to be so today. When this book first appeared people were shocked to read the entry by Archbishop Tutu, Nobel peace prize winner, who contemplated meeting Adolf Hitler and Idi Amin in Heaven. Surely heaven can't be that inclusive? Surely God can't be that generous?

But the God of Jesus *is* that generous. That's why I have included people you might not expect to find together in heaven. William Hague and Tony Blair, for instance, or Mohammed Al Fayed and John Major. There is a place for all ages, races and creeds. I hope that this book will challenge people to see that there might also be a place in heaven for them too.

I have undertaken this book as a Christian, or at least as one who tries to live up to that title. I pray that these pages may stir in you a longing for God and an irrepressible love for your neighbour, bringing earth a little nearer to heaven.

Michael Seed

Thoughts on heaven from the rich, the ...

$\mathcal{A}$cknowledgements

I would like to thank each contributor to this book – those on earth and those now at peace – for taking the time to send me their thoughts on heaven. I thank especially the headmaster and children of Soho Parish School; and the Society of St Paul for giving permission to reproduce extracts from my original book. Annie Tempest and her son, Freddy, Luke Coppen of the *Catholic Herald*, Mark Reeve, Rowel Friers and Michael Heath for the most heavenly cartoons. John Blake for the invitation to edit the book and Graeme Andrew and all at Blake Publishing for creating it. Finally to Noel Botham, one of the most *spiritual* men I know, at his angelic court of the French House, Soho, without whose help this book would have remained very much on earth.

Michael

us, the poor, the needy and the notorious

Thoughts on heaven from the rich, the

Foreword

We all long for heaven where God is, but we have it in our power to be in heaven with Him right now. To be happy with Him now means loving as He loves, giving as He gives, serving as He serves, rescuing as He rescues, touching Him in the distressing disguise of the poorest of the poor by being His presence, His love, His compassion in their lives.

Let us pray for each other that we may be the sunshine of God's love – the hope of eternal happiness to all whose lives we touch daily.

Heaven for me will be the joy of being with Jesus and Mary and all the other saints and angels, and all our poor – all of us going home to God.

Let us ask Jesus and Mary, the saints and angels to pray for us that we do God's work with love and that we do not spoil it – the beauty of God's work.

Father Michael has compiled this book and I am sure it will do great good to the glory of God and peace in the world. Keep the joy of loving God in your heart and share this joy with all you meet. Let us pray.

God bless you.

Mu Teresa m

Mother Teresa MC
Mother Teresa of the Missionaries of Charity, Calcutta, wrote this foreword before her death in 1997. It is retained as a tribute to her many remarkable achievements in pursuing God's work on earth and asking her prayers from heaven.

us, the poor, the needy and the notorious

The Innocent Wisdom of Children

Leon: Some people don't believe in Heaven.
Sarah: And they go down to hell ... that's where the devil is.
Edmund: I don't know if there is a devil.
Denzil: Heaven is a place where animals don't bite!

A discussion between eight-year-old children at Burdett-Couts & Townshend Foundation School, Westminster.

This conversation inspired Father Michael to compile the original book.

Thoughts on heaven from the rich, the

Heaven...

And Love

us, the poor, the needy and the notorious

BUCKINGHAM PALACE

Dear Father Seed,

A sense of wellbeing, of peace with the world and humanity steals over you the minute you set foot in your boat. You are the master and can forget your work and the troubles of the world. You become a part of your ship, graceful as a bird, skimming effortlessly over the waves, testing your skill, not against anyone else's but against nature, your ideals and the person you would like to be.

Sailing on a sunny day, with a fresh breeze blowing, with maybe somebody you really care for, is the nearest thing to heaven I will ever get on this earth.

HRH Princess Anne, The Princess Royal

Thoughts on heaven from the rich, the f

us, the poor, the needy and the notorious

ANTHONY HOPKINS

Dear Fr. Michael,

If I enter Heaven, I hope to be galvanised by the sudden revelation of a truth we have always subconciously known — that this whole life has been a dream, an illusion — and then have a great chortle at the joke of it all.

All good wishes,

Anthony Hopkins

ACTOR

Thoughts on heaven from the rich, the

us, the poor, the needy and the notorious

1O DOWNING STREET
LONDON SW1A 2AA

THE PRIME MINISTER

Dear Father Michael,

Heaven is a place you share with others, where there is comfort and peace finally from all the struggles, anxieties and tragedies of worldly life. Where there is good and no evil.

Tony Blair

PRIME MINISTER

Thoughts on heaven from the rich, the

is. the poor. the needy and the notorious

John M. Templeton
Box N-7776, Lyford Cay, Nassau, Bahamas

Dear Father Seed,

Each of us can create here and now our own heaven or hell. The one thing over which we have most control is our own mind.
We can choose to focus on the seven deadly sins which are Pride, Lust, Sloth, Envy, Anger, Covetousness and Gluttony, which are hellish. Or we can focus our minds on the heavenly fruit of the Spirit, which are Love, Joy, Peace, Patience, Kindness, Goodness, Faithfulness, Gentleness and Self-control.

A one-thousand-fold increase in information about reality through science research helps us to understand that Heaven may not be a place above the sky but rather, a development here and now within each human soul. For example, by joyfully giving unlimited love to every human without any exception, our own supply of love is greater after the gift than before and we help to multiply love in the universe. Maybe Saint John described Heaven when he said 'God is love and he who dwells in love, dwells in God and God in him.'

Sincerely yours,

Sir John M. Templeton

PHILANTHROPIST AND FOUNDER OF THE TEMPLETON COLLEGE, OXFORD, THE TEMPLETON FOUNDATION AND SPONSOR FOR THE TEMPLETON PRIZE FOR PROGRESS IN RELIGION

Thoughts on heaven from the rich, the

s. the poor, the needy and the notorious

The Rt Hon Paddy Ashdown MP

HOUSE OF COMMONS
LONDON SW1A 0AA

Dear Father Seed

I don't really count myself much of an expert on Heaven. I probably won't get there, chiefly because I am selfish. But, precisely because I am selfish my idea of Heaven would be to be with my family. We tend to be terribly scattered around the world (I am dictating this just after coming back from a rare visit to France to see my grandson). So, being with them is such a pleasure it would be Heaven to be all together for once.

I would love there to be other people there too. Particularly my friends (and I suppose many of my enemies will be there, but in Heaven that won't matter will it?)

Finally, if my wife is there she would make my life hell if my dog wasn't as well! But, I do quite love him anyway.

With very best wishes.

Yours

Paddy Ashdown

MP AND FORMER LEADER OF THE LIBERAL DEMOCRATS

Thoughts on heaven from the rich, the

s, the poor, the needy and the notorious

Barbara Cartland

Dear Father Michael,

I think your idea is brilliant, and I enclose a poem I wrote a long time ago, which appeared in my book of poems, and I think it is appropriate.

It is so nice nowadays to find anybody who worries about religion.

One thing I know, life can never die,
    Translucent, splendid, flaming like the sun.
Only our bodies wither and deny
    The life force when our strength is done.

Let me transmit this wonderful fire,
    Even a little through my heart and mind,
Bringing the perfect love we all desire,
    To those who seek, yet blindly cannot find.

I have always greatly enjoyed the work of Sir Walter Scott, and I think his words are particularly meaningful,

Love rules the court, the camp, the grove,
And men below, and Saints above;
For Love is Heaven, and Heaven is Love.

With all my very best wishes for a successful book to raise vast sums for your worthy cause.

Dame Barbara Cartland, DBE, DSt J

WRITER

Thoughts on heaven from the rich, the

s, the poor, the needy and the notorious

Thoughts on heaven from the rich, the

DALAI LAMA

Dear Father Michael,

Whether we like it or not, we are all born on this earth as part of one, great human family. Each of us is just a human being like everyone else. Like others, we desire happiness and do not want suffering. Moreover, we all have an equal right to avoid suffering and pursue happiness.

As the end of the twentieth century approaches our world has become smaller and more interdependent. We are united by political and economic ties, linked by worldwide communications. However, we are also drawn together by the problems that confront us: over–population, dwindling natural resources and an environmental crisis that threatens the very existence of the planet that sustains us. Within the context of this new interdependence, self–interest clearly lies in considering the interests of others.

To meet the challenges that face us, we must develop a greater sense of universal responsibility. Each of us must learn to work not just for our own self, family or nation, but for the benefit of all mankind. This need to cooperate can only strengthen the human community.

The sole valid foundation for universal responsibility is love and compassion. Love and compassion are the ultimate source of joy and happiness. Once we recognise their value and actually try to cultivate them, many other good qualities — forgiveness, tolerance, inner strength and confidence to overcome fear and insecurity — come forth naturally. These qualities are essential if we are to create a better, happier, more stable and civilised world.

Although some may dismiss love and compassion as impractical and unrealistic. I believe its practice is the true source of success. Therefore, kindness is not the

s. the poor, the needy and the notorious

responsibility merely of those whose work is to care for others, but the necessary business of every section of the human community.

The most immediate challenge facing us today is that of world peace, but how can we achieve it? Beautiful words are no longer enough. We should instead embark on the difficult task of building an attitude of love and compassion within ourselves. It is evident that in order to establish genuine, lasting world peace, we must first set about creating inner peace.

In this century of rapid advancement, material development has brought with it an undue emphasis on external progress. As a result we often forget to foster the most basic human need for kindness, love, cooperation and caring. Yet, the very development of human society is founded on such a basis. So, preserving our essential humanity involves cultivating a sense of responsibility for our fellow human beings.

Once again it is clear that a genuine sense of responsibility can only come about by developing compassion. Only a spontaneous feeling of empathy with others can really inspire us to act on their behalf. Nevertheless. compassion does not arise simply by ordering it to do so. Such a sincere feeling must grow gradually, cultivated within each individual, based on their own conviction of its worth. Adopting an attitude of kindness and universal responsibility is, then, a personal matter. How we conduct ourselves in daily life is, after all, the real test of our compassion.

His Holiness the Dalai Lama

Thoughts on heaven from the rich, the

NATIONAL SECULAR SOCIETY
(Limited by Guarantee). Registration No. 1418145

FOUNDED 1866 BY
CHARLES BRADLAUGH

HONORARY ASSOCIATES

Dr CYRIL BIBBY   BRIGID BROPHY   Dr FRANCIS CRICK   MICHAEL FOOT MP   LORD HOUGHTON   GEORGE MELLY
LORD RAGLAN   LORD WILLIS   BARONESS WOOTTON

Heaven?

For the vast majority of sentient beings, the world in which we find ourselves certainly leaves a great deal to be desired; why assume, however, that a supposed hereafter, if designed by the same alleged creator, would be any better?

If heaven entailed my indulging such a creator's appetite for adoration, that would be hell! But the whole idea of any conscious life after death is absurd, however much one might desire it – consciousness being possible only in association with a functioning nervous system. So my one personal posthumous hope is that for a few years I may live on in the memories of living friends and in any influence for good that I have achieved in life. And that is enough.

Barbara Smoker.

Barbara Smoker
(Former President of the
National Secular Society 1971-1996)

s. the poor, the needy and the notorious

Heaven…

On Earth

JOHN CLEESE

Dear Father Seed,

I believe I wrote a brief note to you a few days ago on my return from India but our letters appear to have crossed.

I am afraid I am going to decline your invitation, not just because of lack of time but because, on a few minutes contemplation this morning, I realise I have nothing to say!

And, I've learned that under these conditions, it is better to shut up!

Forgive me.

With best wishes.

Yours sincerely

JOHN CLEESE

ACTOR AND COMEDIAN

Thoughts on heaven from the rich, the

...s, the poor, the needy and the notorious

ROY HUDD

Dear Father Michael,

Heaven is the West Country – not my idea but my son's. When he was a toddler and I was away from home doing a summer season in Torquay his bedtime prayer was always:

'Our Father which art in Devon'.

Roy Hudd

COMEDIAN

Thoughts on heaven from the rich, the

TERRY WOGAN

Dear Fr. Michael,

Thank you for your letter, and your warm support!

Herewith, an inadequacy:

The real trouble about getting your <u>Eternal Reward</u> is that you just might get it in the neck in <u>The Other Place</u> as well. If you believe the <u>good</u> will get what's coming to them - then you have to belive it's ditto for the <u>baddie.</u> Otherwise, it doesn't matter if you're Genghis Khan or St. Anthony, you're going <u>UP.</u>

I've always thought that Heaven was here, and Hell, too. And, like the rest of life, <u>Who Gets Which</u> is pretty arbitrary. I've been lucky - my Heaven is on Earth ...

Every success with the tome.

Kindest regards.

Yours sincerely,

Terry Wogan

Terry Wogan.

TV PRESENTER AND DJ

..s, the poor, the needy and the notorious

Genghis Khan, St Antony and
Terry Wogan by Rowel Friers
the leading Irish cartoonist

Thoughts on heaven from the rich, the

...s, the poor, the needy and the notorious...

Dear Father Michael,

My heaven is an interior landscape – not subject to anyone else's frame of reference. It is an eternal now – non-dynamic, non-throphic. Although my heaven will be unique, within I will feel spiritually connected like a single perfect stitch in God's huge tapestry that was, in earthly life, just a lost piece of colourful wool waiting to be threaded and included. In this interior landscape I would be suspended in a state of total fulfilment and peace. My five senses would be active within the eternal now:

Sight: A beautiful meadow, with wild flowers, lavender, trees, hills and a stream. Early morning sunlight.

Sound: The trickling of the stream over stones.

Smell: Lavender and new grass.

Touch: Warm earth.

Taste: Fresh garden mint.

Annie Tempest

Annie Tempest

CARTOONIST

Thoughts on heaven from the rich, the

41

s, the poor, the needy and the notorious

Lambeth Palace
London

Dear Father Michael,

It is in the context of anxieties, lack of hope and such fears about the future, both personal and universal, that we turn to look again at what the Christian faith affirms. The calm and assured message of the Bible does not disregard the realities of which these fears are the expression. But in facing them and interpreting them, it assures us that whatever the future holds, *God is*, and is as Bishop David Jenkins used to say 'as he is in Jesus'. The Christian hope does not depend on an almanac which gives us a date when Christ will return in victory; but it insists that we may rely on it. He *will* return. There *will be* an establishing in totality of his kingdom of love, light and justice, the mode of which can only be glimpsed in picture language. For beyond the Four Last Things – death so familiar and so unyielding, judgement so feared and rebelled against, hell expressing all that is ultimately most negative and destructive, and heaven, that dream of high delight in the immediate presence of God to be enjoyed for ever – beyond even these is the *Last Thing* of all, on which all depends: the immortal and eternal God.

> There, in that other world, what waits for me?
> What shall I find after that other birth?
> Not stormy, tossing, foaming sea,
> But a new earth.
> No sun to mark the changing of the days,
> No slow, soft falling of the alternate night,
> No moon, no star, no light upon my ways,
> Only the Light.
> No gray cathedral, wide and wondrous fair,
> That I may tread where all my fathers trod,
> Nay, nay, my soul, no house of God is there,
> But only God.

Mary Coleridge.

+ George Cantua

George Carey,
Archbishop of Canterbury

Thoughts on heaven from the rich, the

us, the poor, the needy and the notorious

From
PAUL SCOFIELD

Dear Father Seed,

I am most grateful to you for wishing to include a contribution from me for the book "I will see you in Heaven, where the animals don't bite". I wish very much that I could feel that I could contribute with honesty and truth; but my own perception of the hereafter is a blank, albeit a hopeful one, and with no scepticism as to the possibility of Something, some sort of positive continuity which will render death a comma rather than a full-stop. I regret that I cannot visualise any kind of scenario, but I write to you as I feel.

I am grateful for your kind invitation and I wish great success for the book.

Yours sincerely,

Paul Scofield.

ACTOR

Thoughts on heaven from the rich, the

...s, the poor, the needy and the notorious

THOR HEYERDAHL

Tenerife,
Islas Canaries,
Spain

Dear Father Michael,

It is as difficult for me to have any impression about heaven as it is for a blind rain worm to describe the rainbow. The human body and its nervous system is so wisely designed that the full truth is hidden for us in life time when we are prisoners in our own body, with ears and eyes adjusted to let it receive wavelengths of exceedingly limited frequencies.

My kindest regards and best wishes,

Thor Heyerdahl

LEADER OF THE KON-TIKI EXPEDITION

Thoughts on heaven from the rich, the

Dear Father Michael,

Heaven is when the dog next door stops yapping, when the sun shines and the blossom comes out.

Heaven is a seat behind the bowler's arm, an old church at mid wicket, a pub at long leg.

Heaven is a tight knit and loving family; mum and dad, children, uncles and aunts. Nothing beats it. Trust me, I'm a grandad.

Heaven is Astaire dancing, Sinatra singing, Oscar Peterson playing. Heaven is also when the world shuts up and all we hear are the sounds of silence.

I'm not sure I want to go to heaven, even if they'll have me. I might meet too many people I'd rather not live next door to. If they owned a yapping dog I'd be forced to ask for a transfer.

Yours sincerely

Michael Parkinson

BROADCASTER

us, the poor, the needy and the notorious

D A V I D   B E L L A M Y

Dear Father Michael,

When we have all come to our senses and learned to live in harmony with all the products of creative evolution, then there will be heaven on earth. Until that time I must be content with a walk in ancient forest land where I can at least in my mind's eye be with my mum and dad and all my family and friends and, due to the closeness of the purpose of creation, believe that it has already come to pass.

Professor David Bellamy

TV PERSONALITY AND BOTANIST

Thoughts on heaven from the rich, the f

us, the poor, the needy and the notorious

SUGGS

Dear Father Michael,
My Idea of Heaven, in the here, or
the here after. Would be, a clear spring
afternoon, of drifting on the Regents Park
boating lake. The sound of a distant brass band
interrupted by the sploshing of a cold bottle of white
wine appearing though the reeds, on a piece of
string. The scent of blossom, the quaching
of ducks, the woman you love.
All the best
Suggs.

TV PRESENTER AND FORMER LEAD SINGER OF MADNESS

Thoughts on heaven from the rich, the

us, the poor, the needy and the notorious

NEWS _{OF THE} WORLD
BRITAIN'S BIGGEST SELLING NEWSPAPER

FROM THE
EDITOR

1 VIRGINIA STREET
LONDON E1 9XR

Dear Father Michael,

My idea of Heaven would be to edit God's newspaper.   I would have Einstein as my science correspondent, Gladstone as political editor and Bobby Moore as head of the sports department.

And every splash story would be a happy one - what bliss!

Good luck with your book.

Kind regards.

PHILIP HALL

Former Editor,
News of the World

Thoughts on heaven from the rich, the

Heaven…

And Sacrifice

CREATIVE ARTISTS AGENCY, INC.
LITERARY AND TALENT AGENCY

Dear Father Michael,

My thoughts right now are so concentrated on the film at hand that it is difficult for me to formulate any words that I feel worthy.

My very best wishes for success in your venture.

I WILL SEE YOU IN HEAVEN

With my Best wishes

Sean Connery

Sean Connery

ACTOR

Thoughts on heaven from the rich, the

s, the poor, the needy and the notorious

Palais de Monaco

Dear Father Michael,
Please find enclosed a memento of my beloved wife as a token
of my appreciation for your kind message.

O God, grant me the serenity
to accept the things I cannot change,
the courage to change the things I can,
and the wisdom to know the difference.

HIS SERENE HIGHNESS RAINIER III
The Prince Sovereign of Monaco chose this prayer as his contribution.

Thoughts on heaven from the rich, the

West London Mission of the Methodist Church
19 Thayer Street, London W1M 5LJ
Telephone: 0171 935 6179

Dear Father Michael

Looking back over a very long life I am astonished at the comparative indifference of my earlier years to the prospect of life after death. I professed it publicly as a Methodist preacher. I remember that I recited it regularly in my prayers - but like so many human issues it seemed such a long way off that for me it was relatively unimportant.

Now I am an old man, and to put it simply, death is a very 'live' issue and words like heaven and hell have an unavoidable immediacy. In fact I now am convinced it has become an absolute requirement to realise that our human experience on this planet is not the sum total of reality. Unless there is something beyond this earthly realm, 'sound and fury signifying nothing' loom as almost a final verdict on human experience.

All our aspirations as to the quality of life after death, all its anticipation of human relationships restored after being served on earth, all questions about what it will be like for the good, and what it presages for the bad, and above all will I be happy and fulfilled, or disappointed - All this ultimately depends on whether heaven is a 'must or myth'.

I am now satisfied that if there is any truth anywhere, it can only be credible if there is an optimistic future beyond the grave.

To believe and assert that 'God is love' demands a realm of existence where fulfilment of His loving purpose can happen - and it cannot fully happen in the world of time and space and matter. We can and ought to begin the pilgrimage, here and now, to His Kingdom, but we need that eternal world so that those who start out, like Christian in *Pilgrim's Progress*, can not only find the wages of going on from day to day, but can catch the sound of the trumpets that sound for them on the other side.

Yours sincerely

Donald Soper

The Rev. Lord Soper,
former President of the Methodist Conference.
These words were given shortly before his death in 1998.

us, the poor, the needy and the notorious

The Rt Hon the Earl of Longford KG PC

ℋouse of Lords

My dear Father Michael

The best I can manage about Heaven is this:

Groucho Marx said that if a club elected him, he would know that there was something wrong with the club.

I would feel that about Heaven if I arrived there on my departure from this planet. If I looked around and saw that it closely resembled the House of Lords a few years back, I would feel that somewhere along the line I had been seriously misled.

So for me, purgatory is an essential article of faith. I don't say that I can understand what it is like, but I have a much clearer view of it than I have of what, in the House of Lords, they call 'the other place'.

Reading this, I still feel that it represents my deepest feeling about Heaven. But since writing it I have been more and more in contact with men who have committed terrible crimes and I simply cannot believe that a merciful God would pack them off to Hell. In other words, purgatory for all of us except a few Saints, seems to be the inevitable answer. I can easily imagine arriving in front of St. Peter along with my friend of the last few years, Denis Nielsen who was convicted of many murders. I can imagine St. Peter not discriminating too closely between us, particularly in view of the advantages or disadvantages we have received in this life.

So purgatory, the process of purification, is what I expect and hope for. Heaven of course must be the ultimate ideal but it would be impertinent to think of me arriving there in the near future.

With my best wishes

Frank

Longford

PHILANTHROPIST

Thoughts on heaven from the rich, the

is, the poor, the needy and the notorious

KEITH WATERHOUSE

Dear Father Michael —

My idea of heaven:

I should like heaven to be a replica of earth, with all
its flaws and failings though without its woes and wars.
Daily, an immense amount of good is done here on earth,
and those of us who are not good profit by the example
of those who are, so that however intermittently and
incompetently, we occasionally strive to emulate them.
The conventional idea of heaven, where all is perfection,
leaves no scope for goodness — there is nothing to be
good about!

Best wishes

Keith

JOURNALIST AND WRITER

Thoughts on heaven from the rich, the

s. the poor. the needy and the notorious

Dear Father Michael,

To be sailing on a small boat with two of my Donegal mates on a gentle sea, with the sun shining out of a clear blue sky, a few beers in a bag: and to be slowly working our way round Arranmore Island in Co. Donegal before coming back to a nice meal with our families.

Safe in the knowledge that there is no phone in the boat and no one knows where we are and we simply cannot be got at by anyone!

This is Heaven!

Gay Byrne

TV PRESENTER AND DJ

Thoughts on heaven from the rich, the

Sir Sigmund Sternberg
Charitable Foundation

Star House 104-108 Grafton Road
London NW5 4BD

Dear Father Michael,

My idea of a perfect heaven is that of a place that provides space for people: emotional space to develop their hearts and attitudes, and physical space to train and relax their muscles. I visualise a huge mirror, just slightly distorted to make one laugh at oneself, and develop a sense of humour. There should be bicycles and skipping ropes, and that mirror will show clearly that despite all efforts to keep moving we do look slightly ridiculous. Only thus can we develop patience with ourselves and others and achieve that inner glow that comes from the happy feeling of having tried to do better.

Sir Sigmund Sternberg
Chairman, Executive Committee of the
International Council of Christians and Jews

BUSINESSMAN AND FOUNDER OF THE THREE FAITHS FORUM

s. the poor, the needy and the notorious

From: The Rt Hon John Major MP

HOUSE OF COMMONS
LONDON SW1A 0AA

Dear Father Michael,

On this occasion, I thought perhaps a less serious contribution may be appropriate.

Those who know me, and many who do not, know that I love cricket. I always have done. I love the charm and the grace of the game. Its unpredictability. Its history. Its literature. Its essential Englishness. It is one of England's greatest exports. A game not only played around the civilised world – but one that can truly claim to have helped to civilise it.

Thus my own personal 'Heaven on Earth' would be to open the batting for England at the Oval and to score a double century. Before a car crash in Nigeria ruled this particular vision of paradise out of the question, if Our Lord had offered the choice of becoming Prime Minister or of captaining England, it would have been a very hard decision to make!

With best wishes

Yours sincerely,
John Major

MP AND FORMER PRIME MINISTER

Thoughts on heaven from the rich, the

s, the poor, the needy and the notorious

Heaven…

In Heaven

James Herbert

Dear Fr. Michael,

I took a break in writing to get my piece on Heaven to you. I must admit, I thoroughly enjoyed the exercise!

I hope it's usable.

My idea of Heaven? Broad expanses of green lawns, neat, cultured gardens, lush woodlands in the distance leading to rolling hills, which in turn lead to pale blue, ice-topped mountains, all this beneath an azure, cloudless sky, with the sounds of birds singing and fountains whispering softly filling the air. There are never too many people around but those who do stroll this calm paradise are of beatific nature and gracious disposition; they wear flowing white robes. A feeling of tranquillity and wellbeing is all-pervading, aches, pains and troubles are gone, thoughts are clear and full of gentle though awesome energy, the ability to visit the universe, and an understanding of all the mysteries is within our providence. Love will be everywhere in the souls you meet, in the very nature of the environment around you, and in yourself; and it will be a love without negative extremes – no passion, no jealousy, no despair – a love that just *is*.

Okay, so that's my ideal of Heaven, a fantasy shared, I would guess, by millions of like-minded romanticists. The actuality? Who knows? Who really has the faintest idea? I believe it's a concept beyond all our imaginations, one that is bound to lose credence the moment it *is* conceptualised. The mystery of Faith declares that it should be so, life itself an important but small piece of the jigsaw. To know the answer (the complete picture) would negate the value of that piece, for ultimate knowledge must come with the joining.

My guess – and it's only a guess – is that we take much of ourselves with us when we leave our physical body: memories, learning (or even lack of), and of course, most importantly, our spirit. Death could never be a state of mind, but it could be a state of spirit.

I think our images of Heaven, versions told by those of us who have had near-death experience, or those with visions or dreams of such a place, could well have some truth to them. The journey down a long tunnel at

Thoughts on heaven from the rich, the

the end of which is a bright light, the feeling of peace and the absence of pain, the welcoming of friends or relations who have gone before us, there to comfort and acclimatize us to our new state: all could be part of the process that allows that which we already know to blend smoothly with that which we are about to learn, a kind of instructional half-way house, if you like, that reassuringly mixes perceived reality with the first of further understanding.

I think that we become part of the whole again (perhaps that jigsaw analogy, as simple as it is, serves its purpose here), a whole that we leave but from which we are never truly disconnected (we're still part of the main picture) when we are born. While remaining individual, eventually we are absorbed into everything that is, ever was, and ever will be. Yes, I believe we are free to explore the universe, and other universes besides, and our quest for ultimate truth continues until we reach the next level (of which there are many) of higher understanding. And where is it all leading? Simply, to the power we know as God.

So, my thoughts are that Heaven is a glorious and magnificent metaphor for an after existence we all seek either overtly or covertly (and perhaps even unknowingly) and one that probably we are all – or nearly all – destined for despite our faults and misdemeanours in this world. Naturally, I could be wrong; but then, so could everybody else.

My best wishes to you and all the wonderful work you do.

Yours sincerely

James Herbert

WRITER

s, the poor, the needy and the notorious

Thoughts on heaven from the rich, the

Billy Graham
Evangelistic Association

Dear Father Seed,

The Christian hope is based on two worlds – this world and the next. When these two worlds are in view, we are adequately prepared for a full life here. The Christian has the hope of a life of joy, peace, and outgoing love in the midst of a world of trouble. The Christian has the hope of better living conditions as a result of Christian influence in any society or community. However, the Christian's great and ultimate hope is in the world to come.

Everything in respect to heaven will be new. It is described as a new creation in which we shall move in new bodies, possessed of new names, singing new songs, living in a new city, governed by a new form of government, and challenged by new prospects of eternity. The paradise that man lost will be regained, but it will be much more. It will be a new paradise, not the old one repaired and made over. When God says, 'Behold, I make all things new,' the emphasis is on 'all things.' We shall live in a brand-new world.

Heaven will be the perfection we have always longed for. All the things that made earth unlovely and tragic will be absent in heaven. There will be no night, no death, no disease, no sorrow, no tears, no ignorance, no disappointment, no war. It will be filled with health, vigor, virility, knowledge, happiness, worship, love, and perfection.

Heaven will be more modern and up to date than any of the present-day constructions of man. Heaven will be a place to challenge the creative genius of the unfettered mind of redeemed man. Heaven will be a place made supremely attractive by the presence of Christ.

However, the most thrilling thing to me about heaven is that Jesus Christ will be there. I will see Him face to face. I will have the opportunity to talk directly to Him and to ask Him a hundred questions that I have never had answered.

Sometimes we get a little tired of the burdens of life, but it is exhilarating to know that Jesus Christ will meet us at the end of life's journey.

s, the poor, the needy and the notorious

Billy Graham
Evangelistic Association

The joy of being with Him for ever is beyond the ability of any writer to describe. There is only one way to heaven. Jesus said: 'I am the way, the truth, and the life: no man cometh unto the Father but by me' (Jn. 14:6).

The last invitation of the Bible says: 'And the Spirit and the bride say, Come. And let him that heareth say, Come. And let him that is athirst come. And whosoever will, let him take the water of life freely' (Rev. 22:17).

This is still an age of grace. God's offer of forgiveness and a new life still stands. However, the door will one day be closed. Someday it will be too late. This is why the Bible continually warns and challenges: 'Now is the accepted time' (11Co. 6:2).

Gratefully in Christ,

Billy Graham

Evangelist

Thoughts on heaven from the rich, the

Noel Botham

Growing up in Yorkshire I heard many references to Heaven and Hell and most of them had to do with the here and now and in particular, it seemed then, with the ups and downs of family life.

Husbands are in heaven whose wives don't scold. Marriages are made in heaven - and often lived out in hell. Brides were in seventh heaven - but, oh, so briefly. Then they were heard telling husbands that hell would never be full until they, the men, were in it.

Other wives would console one another with the adage that those who live permanently in hell think there is no other heaven.

And all Yorkshiremen, it appeared, entreated the good Lord, on a daily basis, to deliver them from the ravages of Hell, Hull and Halifax. Hell seemed highly unattractive and most folk expected only transient stays in heaven ...

Then I heard of the paradise I best remember from my childhood days in Osbaldwick. It is a very special heaven which takes care of just bairns and drunk men.

Having never properly grown up and at the same time increasingly enjoying the pleasures of drinking fine wines and champagnes I find myself more and more counting on this exclusive heaven existing.

Tucked up in bed as a child I was told by Nanny that one was chosen for heaven by being touched by an angel.

I hope my favourite heaven has an angel who will be sent to touch us and let us know it is time to be whisked away.

Then to join old friends in a childlike, bacchanalian celebration that lasts for all eternity.

Noel Botham
Author

us, the poor, the needy and the notorious

Dear Father Michael,

I am afraid that I have little to say on the subject of Heaven, but you might care for a quotation from the Book of Revelations – a quotation which I have often read from the pulpit – a good political quote!

AND I SAW A NEW HEAVEN AND A NEW EARTH:
FOR THE FIRST HEAVEN AND THE FIRST EARTH WERE PASSED AWAY.

You will see that I did not finish the quotation - we are rather fond of the sea!

You might like to use the poem which my wife wrote about Heaven, a poem which John Betjeman greatly liked.

Yours sincerely

Wilson of Rievaulx

THE LATE FORMER PRIME MINISTER AND MP

Thoughts on heaven from the rich, the

us, the poor, the needy and the notorious

Dear Father Seed,

Here is my poem about Heaven, which you might care to include;

Or you might prefer my so far unpublished poem for John Betjeman?

Best wishes,

Yours sincerely,

Mary Wilson.

Mary Wilson

POET

Thoughts on heaven from the rich, the

There must be somewhere, where the children live
Who die in pain, asking their mothers why?
Some far-off place, untroubled by our tears,
Where they may travel through their stolen years
And lost maturity?

Will those, in battle or in accident
Blasted from a life, no time to say a prayer,
Awaken to tranquillity, and find
The suicides, the handicapped and blind
Restored to wholeness there?

And to that country, shall we come at last,
From life, through death, come once again to live
And know at last the reason for our pain,
And those we loved and wounded, see again
And ask them to forgive?

Our childhood images may disappear -
No stern Saint Peter waiting with his keys
To open pearly gates on streets of gold,
No shining angels will their wings unfold
To greet us; none of these,

But such a peace as we have never known,
And such a light as here has never shone
Unless we glimpsed it in the afterglow
On summer Sunday evenings long ago
After the sun had gone.

O Spirit whence we came, it must be so,
It must be so, O God whom we adore!
You would not thrust us into endless sleep,
Into a nothingness so vast, so deep
That we are lost for evermore?

Mary Wilson.

is, the poor, the needy and the notorious

To John Betjeman, on his arrival in Heaven.

Are you easy, John, beneath the shining towers?
Do you stand, uncertain, by the pearly gate?
Does the light of glory shine beyond the walls
Where you wait?

There's a hum of voices round the sapphire throne,

And the sound of footsteps on the streets of gold
As your joyful friends reach out to draw you in
To the fold.

Mary Wilson

To John Betjeman, on his arrival in Heaven.

Are you easy, John, beneath the shining towers?
Do you stand, uncertain, by the pearly gates?
Does the light of glory shine beyond the walls
Where you wait?

There's a hum of voices round the sapphire throne,
And the sound of footsteps on the streets of gold
As your joyful friends reach out to draw you in
To the fold.

Mary Wilson
Written in memory of the Poet Laureate, John Betjeman.

Thoughts on heaven from the rich, the

THE LEONARD CHESHIRE FOUNDATION INTERNATIONAL

From: Group Captain Leonard Cheshire VC OM DSO DFC

Dear Father Richard,

Last year's Festival of Remembrance in the Albert Hall in London suddenly seemed to have a little message for me about our death. In the centre is the large arena on which the action takes place, and round it, tier upon tier of spectators, a cross-section of the nation with the Queen at their head. The action mostly consists of displays by the armed forces, but others enter the stage too - somebody who was wounded in the war, some ex-nursing auxiliaries, a land army girl, a widow and so on. They are first announced, then enter via a short tunnel and down some steps and everybody's straining to see them, clapping and cheering as they walk across the arena.

Well, in a tiny way, I think that's a mirror of the day we enter heaven. The moment of our dying is an extremely solemn moment, it's a moment of the most profound possible meaning, not just to us but to the myriads and myriads who already inhabit heaven, who see it as a marvellous victory - of Christ who made it possible, but also of us who, too, paid a price. You could even say there's a third victory, of all those who've helped us on our way. Each person who enters heaven adds to the joy of everybody else there. So different from our attitude on earth!

Best wishes,

Leonard Cheshire

**Founder of the Cheshire Homes.
Lord Cheshire gave these words
shortly before his death.**

us, the poor, the needy and the notorious

ARCHBISHOP DESMOND TUTU

Dear Father Seed,

I once read a two volume work entitled *The Faith of a Moralist* by A. Taylor. I really remember little of what I read except a fascinating and indeed compelling image of heaven and it was this.

The author said in Heaven we will have no time for jealousy because we will all be so engrossed in the beauty that is God, discovering ever new levels of beauty in God who is the Infinite One. And like lovers or those who have discovered something beautiful, we would want others to share in the beauty, the loveliness, the holiness that we had seen and they in their turn would be eager to share with us what they had so ecstatically found.

There would thus be this discovery and eagerness to share forever and ever, because God is an infinity of beauty, goodness and love – a love that I believe would ultimately be compellingly irresistible.

I wonder what we would do if we discovered a Hitler or an Amin in Heaven - they having found God's love quite irresistible?

Archbishop Desmond Tutu
Retired Archbishop of Cape Town, R.S.A.
and winner of the Nobel Peace Prize.

Thoughts on heaven from the rich, the

us, the poor, the needy and the notorious

CHRIS PATTEN

My dear Father Michael,

My idea about heaven is ... time; time to spend with each member of my family and my friends; enjoy and build on my relationship with them; time to read all the books that I've spent my life putting on one side because it was going to take too much effort to tackle them; time to go on very long walks and look at and learn about the trees and the wild flowers and the shrubs along the way; time to stand for long enough in front of paintings to enjoy and understand them; time to sit down and concentrate while listening to great music; time to think - to think about nothing particular - and time to pray.

Best wishes and a happy Christmas.

Yours sincerely

The Rt. Hon. Christopher Patten C.H.
The last Governor of Hong Kong

Thoughts on heaven from the rich, the f

us. the poor, the needy and the notorious

RUTH RENDELL

Dear Father Michael,

I liked Denzil's definition of Heaven very much. In one of my books I said, or had a character say, that a heaven for cats would be a hell for mice, and this isn't quite as frivolous as it sounds. Heaven for me would have no football in it but that would be hell for Sir Geoff Hurst or David Beckham; another protagonist of mine imagined Heaven to be an enormously expanded version of the London Library, hell for those who never read; my celestial city must look and feel like Venice: what of those who prefer Glasgow?

So we had better not conceive of Heaven in these terms. Seeing God, we are told, union with God in peace and glory. That will do all right for me.

With best wishes,

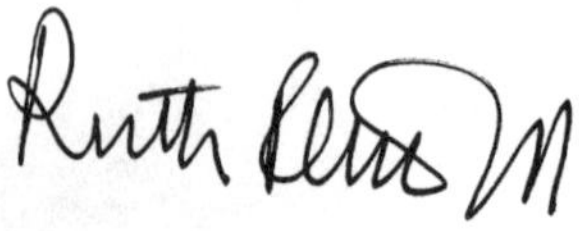

Ruth Rendell

WRITER

us, the poor, the needy and the notorious

ARCHBISHOP'S HOUSE,

WESTMINSTER, LONDON, SW1P 1QJ

Dear Michael,

I submit the following reflection:

St John, who well understood the strength and warmth of God's love for us, asks: 'How can a man with no love have any knowledge of God, since God is love? I believe that through the experience of human love a person comes to have some concept, some idea, of what love is like in God.

So all those times when we have been drawn to others by the goodness and lovableness which we have discovered in them, are precious experiences. They are hints given to us by God of the way He thinks of us.

I see this life as a period of training, a time of preparation, during which we learn the art of loving God and our neighbour, which is the heart of the Gospel message, sometimes succeeding, sometimes failing. As we learn, then many things begin to look different.

Death, for instance, comes to be seen as the way which leads us to the vision of God, the moment when we shall see Him as He really is, and find our total fulfilment in love's final choice. The ultimate union with that which is most lovable, union with God. I call that the moment of ecstasy.

Basil Hume

Cardinal Basil Hume O.S.B.
Archbishop of Westminster

Thoughts on heaven from the rich, the

© Jesper di John, Switzerland.

us, the poor, the needy and the notorious

Dear Father Michael,

There are so many things I will look forward to seeing in heaven.
Presuming I will get there (let me know if you have heard
anything different from the big boss!)
Here are a few of them...

Trees that grow curly wurlies
Taps that flow with chilled Vimto
Flamenco around a camp fire
Reunions with dear ones who have gone before
Even better jokes
Laughter
Seeing people who I thought would never get in!
Above all... Happiness

Love

Fiona Allen

FIONA ALLEN

ACTRESS

Thoughts on heaven from the rich, the

ESSEX
ENGLAND

My dear father Michael,

My idea about heaven would be to meet in person, Bessie Smith,
Janis Joplin and Ernest Hemingway. Three idols in one room.
It would be a dark stormy night and there would be a roaring
fire, a decanter or two of brandy and I would listen enthralled as
they talked, reminisced about their lives, and told me their
darkest secrets. Janis Joplin and Bessie Smith would sing,
Ernest Hemingway would discuss his books and I would sit
back in my seat hanging on every word and feeling very
privileged just to be there.

Much love
Martina Cole

Martina Cole.

AUTHOR

s. the poor, the needy and the notorious

Professor the Lord Alton of Liverpool

House of Lords
London SW1A 0PW

Dear Father Michael,

In the past decade I have watched my father and mother die and been blessed by the birth of two more children, Philip and James.

Endings and beginnings are sharp reminders of our mortality and the uselessness of most of the baggage which we accumulate. In these moments of heightened joy and grief we can best understand the promise of the psalmist that 'I have known you even before I created you in your mother's womb.'

Heaven will be a time of renewed acquaintance with parents, lost children, and relatives of every generation. There will be no pain or suffering, only joy, light and healing.

C S Lewis knew all this when he wrote so convincingly in *The Last Battle* that the adventures of Narnia had only been the cover and the title page: 'Now at last they were beginning Chapter One of the Great Story which no one on earth has read; which goes on for ever; in which every chapter is better than the one before.'

In heaven every chapter will be better than the one before.

Yours ever,

David Alton.

P.s. Hopefully, I'll see you in Heaven, if not before.

Director: The Foundation for Citizenship, Liverpool John Moores University

Thoughts on heaven from the rich, the

In the outside world Heaven and wishful thinking seem to go together.

Heaven for me is to be healthy, happy and contented, not hungry -
happy children - laughter - giving and receiving love - having no enemies
and having great sex - therefore I cannot see the point in dying as I
already have everything that makes my Heaven.

PETER J. STRINGFELLOW

Stringfellows, 16-19 Upper St. Martin's Lane, Covent Garden, London WC2H 9EF Web www.stringfellows.co.uk
Stringfellows is the trading name of Stringfellow Restaurants Ltd. Cabaret of Angels is the trading name of Cabaret of Angels Ltd. Registered Offices 235 Marylebone Road, London NW1 5Q1 Registered No. 2090397 England.

s. the poor, the needy and the notorious

Heaven…

And Light

Dear Father Michael,

I have often wondered whether Heaven might be like Harrods on Christmas Eve when customers and staff alike are full of happiness, notwithstanding the work they have had to put in to ensure other people's well-being. Though they may be weary and a little footsore, everyone has that inner glow of contentment knowing that the struggle is now over and the real pleasure is about to begin. There is an air of joyful anticipation and a sense of relief that anything which has been left undone, did not matter anyway.

My hope is only that I will be able to meet again all the people I have loved and lost over the years and spend a few minutes of eternity with them sitting on a passing cloud, thinking about how much fun it was to have known each other when we were in that state known as 'being alive', even though it lasted only for the blinking of an eye.

Yours sincerely

Mr M. Al Fayed
Chairman

BUSINESSMAN AND CHAIRMAN OF HARRODS

Thoughts on heaven from the rich, the

s, the poor, the needy and the notorious

HOUSE OF COMMONS
LONDON SW1A 0AA

LEADER OF THE OPPOSITION

Dear Father Seed,

I hope that heaven will be like the feeling that I get when I reach the summit after a strenuous hill walk. There is a sense of exhilaration and fulfilment coupled with a sensation of inner peace and wonder at the newly revealed view from the hilltop.

Yr wevely

with Hope.

The Rt Hon William Hague MP

LEADER OF THE CONSERVATIVE PARTY

Thoughts on heaven from the rich, the

s, the poor, the needy and the notorious

claire rayner

Dear Father Seed,

      Thank you for inviting me to take part in your book but I'm afraid this is not a thing with which I can help. As an extremely thoughtful and, if I may say so, ethical atheist I couldn't possibly lie enough to persuade people to believe there is such a place as "heaven". I am sorry.

      Yours sincerely

      Claire Rayner

JOURNALIST AND AGONY AUNT

Thoughts on heaven from the rich, the

s, the poor, the needy and the notorious

DAVID LINLEY FURNITURE LIMITED

Dear Father Michael,

Thank you for your invitation to tell you what heaven means to me, it is the anticipation of calm and rest; a pure and endless dream. Thank you for writing to me and I wish you every success with the new edition.

Yours truly, David Linley

Thank you for your invitation to tell you what heaven means to me, it is the anticipation of calm and rest; a pure and endless dream. Thank you for writing to me and I wish you every success with the new edition.

CARPENTER AND FURNITURE MAKER

Thoughts on heaven from the rich, the

ALTHORP

Dear Father Michael,

Thank you for your letter, asking me to contribute to your book.

I believe heaven to be a place where the dignity of the human soul can prosper. All the concerns that cloud us here, on earth, will not only seem less significant; they will be forgotten completely.

Yours sincerely,

Earl Spencer

CHARLES, 9TH EARL SPENCER

s, the poor, the needy and the notorious

Father Michael Seed

National Spinal Injuries Centre

at Stoke Mandeville Hospital
Mandeville Road, Aylesbury, Bucks HP21 8AL

Father Michael Seed
St Francis Friary
47 Francis Street
Westminster
London SW1P 1 QR

I hope that Heaven will be a mix of all the marvellous people and places I have enjoyed on earth.

To have been born in a place and time that one could see the sky, mountains, waterfalls and some equally lovely people is Heaven on earth. It had better be like that 'upstairs' otherwise I will come back.

SIR JIMMY SAVILE Kt., OBE., KCSG.

TV PERSONALITY AND CHARITY WORKER

Thoughts on heaven from the rich, the

s, the poor, the needy and the notorious

FROM THE OFFICE OF FREDERICK FORSYTH

Dear Father Michael,

Thank you for your letter which just reached me.
Here we go:-

Thirty years ago this summer I found myself walking through fields carpeted edge to edge with small, dying African children. They were the children of Biafra. They screamed, muled, moaned and cried from hunger and malnutrition as the life ebbed out of them

I suppose there must be a place where people do not treat other people like that, nor as in Bosnia, Rwanda, Burundi, East Timor Tibet and Sudan.

I suppose there must be a place where people treat others with kindness, decency, courtesy, humour, compassion, forbearance, generosity and mercy.

It is rather a long list, probably too long for this planet, so I suppose that place must be Heaven.
Hope it will do.

Yours sincerely

Frederick Forsyth

WRITER

Thoughts on heaven from the rich, the

s, the poor, the needy and the notorious

Heaven…

And Life

Dudley Moore

Dear Father Michael,

As I don't believe in God, it is hard for me to believe in heaven … except as we know it on earth! I suppose I would like to stress the immediacy of heaven, since I'm not a believer… so what other choice do I have! It seems almost that one can have an even more startlingly vivid notion of heaven, if one is a non-believer… because we do know (quite certainly) this is all we have!

Dudley Moore

ACTOR AND MUSICIAN

Thoughts on heaven from the rich, the f

us. the poor. the needy and the notorious

Dear Father Seed

I am not sure that my imagination will get me as far as some of the other quotes which you will already have - but I will do my best!

My idea of Heaven is an early morning on a Summer's day in the country in England, before the leaves of the trees have lost their fresh green and the birds are singing and, but for the birds there is total silence. Before the aeroplanes start their continual buzzing and before the tractor and the chain saws get going. There can be nothing more beautiful and peaceful than the English countryside in these conditions, indeed, it is Heaven.

With best wishes

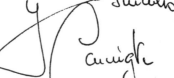

Lord Carrington

FORMER FOREIGN SECRETARY

Thoughts on heaven from the rich, the

GRAHAM GREENE

Dear Father Seed,

Reaching for the wall, Juan turned and began to pray – not for himself, but for his enemies, for the squad of poor innocent Indian soldiers who faced him and even for the Chief of Police himself. He raised the crucifix at the end of his beads and prayed that God would forgive them, would enlighten their ignorance, and bring them at last – as Saul the persecutor was brought – into His eternal kingdom ...

The officer gave the command to present arms. In that moment a smile of complete adoration and happiness passed over Juan's face. It was as if he could see the arms of God open to receive him. He had always told his mother and sisters that he had a premonition that he would be in heaven before them. He would say with a whimsical smile to his mother, the good but over careful housewife: 'I will have tided everything up for you.' Now the moment had come, the officer gave the order to fire ...

Juan, raising both arms above his head, called out in a strong brave voice to the soldiers and the levelled rifles, 'Hail, Christ the King.' Next moment he fell riddled with a dozen bullets and the officer, stooping over his body, put his revolver close to Juan's ear and pulled the trigger ...

No need to have fired another shot. The soul of the young hero had already left its earthly mansion, and the happy smile on the dead face told even those ignorant men where they would find Juan now.

All good wishes to your work and to yourself.
Yours ever,

Graham Greene

Taken from *The Power and the Glory* by Graham Greene.
Sending his signature to authorise the inclusion of this passage
was one of Graham Greene's last acts before his death.

AUTHOR

s. the poor, the needy and the notorious

JOHN GIELGUD

If it be now, 'tis not to come,
if it be not to come it will be now,
if it be not now, yet it will come.
The readiness is all. Since no man
hath aught of what he leaves,
what is't to leave betimes?
Let be.

Hamlet V ii

Heaven
Dear friends. Beauty in house and garden. The changing of the seasons. Music, especially Bach, Mozart, Purcell, Chopin. Fellowship in work, colleagues old and new. Vivid memories thankfully stored up. Hopes continuing. Animal devotion.

Hell
Miseries of the world – wars, disease, starvation, poverty. Desolating outlook – sickness and death of loved friends. Fear of illness and loss of memory. Inability to communicate: diminution of faculties. Misgivings and reluctance to tackle new problems, and increasing distrust of ability to enjoy more than a few people at a time. Shame at self-centredness and past mistakes and sins never forgotten.

Paradise
Wonderful parents and upbringing. The marvels of great literature, especially Shakespeare. A long career in the profession I chose, and the inestimable blessing of having worked with great artists and travelled in so many parts of the world engaged in projects that brought me so much fascination and discovery over so many years.

John Gielgud.

ACTOR

Thoughts on heaven from the rich, the

s, the poor, the needy and the notorious

JOHN GIELGUD

'I'll see you in Heaven'

If it be now, 'tis not to come.
If it be not to come it will be now,
If it be not now, yet it will come.
The readiness is all. Since no man
hath aught of what he leaves
what is't to leave betimes
Let be.

Heaven.

> Dear friends. Beauty in house and garden.
> The changing of the Seasons. Music. especially
> Bach, Mozart, Purcell. Chopin. Fellowship
> in work. colleagues old and new. Vivid
> memories thankfully stored up. Hopes
> continuing. animal devotion.

Hell.

> Miseries of the World. wars, disease, starvation.
> poverty. Desolating outlook. sickness and
> death of loved friends. Fear of illness and
> loss of memory. Inability to communicate;
> diminution of faculties. misgivings and
> reluctance to tackle new problems and
> increasing distrust of ability to enjoy
> more than a few people at a time. shame
> at self-centredness and past mistakes
> and sins. never forgotten.

Paradise.

> Wonderful parents and upbringing.
> The marvels of great Literature. especially
> Shakespeare. A long career in the
> profession I chose and the inestimable
> blessing of having worked with great
> artists and travelled in so many
> parts of the World engaged in work projects
> that brought me so much fascination
> and discovery over so many years.

John Gielgud.

Thoughts on heaven from the rich, the

MICHAEL BLAKEMORE

Dear Father Michael

'I'm in heaven when I'm dancing cheek to cheek,' sang Fred Astaire, and most theologians would dispute his definition of the place we would all prefer to go to. However, being caught up in the spell of a great performer, like Astaire, can certainly be Heavenly. You watch him dance and there's nothing else you'd prefer to be doing. This goes for other things, pieces of music or the pages of certain books. They offer you a fleeting outline of what perfection might be. I had a childhood growing up by the Pacific, and there have been days when the ocean also seemed to offer a happiness outside time. Human concerns and struggles melt away, and you just marvel.

In Heaven the waves would be a perfect blue and white, Bach would be playing and, of course, Fred Astaire would be dancing, though not necessarily to the Bach.

My very best wishes

FILM AND THEATRICAL DIRECTOR

s, the poor, the needy and the notorious

C A M E R O N

M A C K I N T O S H
L I M I T E D

Dear Father Seed,

Unlike most people who have to wait until they die to get to heaven, I have managed to enjoy living there from time to time whilst still on earth. For the most of my life I have had the privilege of enjoying visiting Loch Nevis on the West Coast of Scotland. One day I stumbled on a lovely old map of this area and to my surprise and delight discovered that where Loch Nevis was marked it had written beside it the word 'heaven' just as the neighbouring Loch Hourn was marked 'hell'. Like the real thing, it is impossible to overstate the beauty of this place, containing spectacular scenery and equally spectacular local characters. Also it contains a simple but lovely old disused Catholic church which, at the mass for the rededication of the building as a walkers' bothy, the assembled congregation were told by the irrepressible and irreplaceable local priest, Father Michael, that though this was still the House of God He would have to share it in future – and the ceilidh should now begin! Father Michael is much beloved in the locality and is someone who firmly believes that the Holy Spirit should not be confined to the baptismal font and should be at least 49% proof!

I am sure the real Heaven will be even better but if I am lucky enough to get there, God's going to have His work cut out!

I do hope the piece I have done about Heaven will suit and that you are not related to my local parish priest! In the Heaven that I am writing about the animals certainly do bite and they are called midgies!

Every success for your book.

With kindest regards,

Cameron Mackintosh

IMPRESARIO

Thoughts on heaven from the rich, the

The New York Times
NEW YORK, N.Y. 10036

Dear Father Seed,

Until I received your letter I had not given much serious thought to Heaven. As a journalist, it seems that most of my concerns center around the lives and fortunes of those least likely to make that particular voyage. But I cannot resist the temptation to participate in this volume. So here goes.

I have never completely convinced myself that there is life after death and that the good will go to Heaven and the bad elsewhere. Rather, I am inclined to believe that it is how we lead our lives, and how that, in turn, is reflected in the memories of others that creates our Heaven or Hell, not in some afterlife but now – on a day-to-day basis.

But if the Lord in his wisdom proves me wrong and welcomes to Heaven those who deserve it, I do hope that I shall be included and that, among other things, I shall renew old friendships with long-gone family pets of better disposition.

With all best wishes,

Sincerely.

ARTHUR OCHS SULZBERGER
The late publisher of the New York Times

s, the poor, the needy and the notorious

118

Thoughts on heaven from the rich, the

STRUAN RODGER

Dear Father Michael,
John Arlott on the wireless: 'Not so much a stumping, more a Wiltshire yeoman slaughtering a pig'.
On to Ward's Irish House, Piccadilly, on a Thursday; needlessly squalid, full of sunny people in a shady place; a bacon and cabbage day. Creamy Guiness, spitting wit and a lock-in.
My idea of Heaven.

Struan h Rodger

ACTOR

s, the poor, the needy and the notorious

Heaven…

And Faith

SHAUKAT KHANUM MEMORIAL TRUST

Dear Father Michael,

As a Muslim I believe that the human mind was not made to comprehend Hell or Heavens. Although the Qur'an gives some idea of the splendours of Heavens, yet it goes on to say that it is beyond human imagination.

It will be better than the greatest feeling of happiness we have ever felt.

Best wishes,

Imran Khan

CRICKETER AND POLITICIAN

Thoughts on heaven from the rich, the

us, the poor, the needy and the notcrious

Sir Derek Jacobi

It would indeed be heavenly to know now – beyond any doubt – what, if anything, happens to us after death.

It would indeed be heavenly to know now –
beyond any doubt – what, if anything, happens
to us after death.

ACTOR

Thoughts on heaven from the rich, the

us, the poor, the needy and the notorious

SENATOR J. WILLIAM FULBRIGHT

Dear Father Michael,

My first reaction to the question is that I don't need a heaven after life, that my idea of heaven is time with my wife here on earth. To be serious, I think that what heaven 'looks like', if it looks like anything, is relatively unimportant. Of primary concern to me is that if it exists, it should be a place of peace, a collection of inquiring minds, a community of compatible souls.

Best wishes,

Senator J. William Fulbright
The late Democrat Senator for Arkansas 1945-74

Thoughts on heaven from the rich, the f

The Family at Christ House

Dear Father Michael
One of our residents kindly wrote this for you:

I liked him.
I liked him right away.
We prayed together last night before we went to bed.

We couldn't turn off the air conditioner.
He was sniffling; so I asked him, 'Are you alright?'
He said, 'Not too good.'
I said, 'If we pray, maybe you'll be better.'

We didn't hold hands or anything.
He said he didn't know how to pray.
I told him when you talk from the heart,
It will come through no matter what you feel.
I felt a spiritual uplifting.

I think he was ready;
He had a smile on his face.
They went to get the doctor; at 6.05 he died

He didn't die alone;
You got to acknowledge: he exists in your heart.

James Lindsay
Director

The Family at Christ House
By courtesy of Christ House, Washington. D.C. which is
a hospital for the homeless and
part of the ministry of The Church of The Saviour,
an ecumenical community founded in 1947.

us, the poor, the needy and the notorious

Kate Bush

Dear Father Michael,

Some say that heaven is hell,
Some say that hell is heaven …

In my dome of ivory: a home of activity;
I want the answers quickly;
but I don't have no energy;
I hold a cup of wisdom,
but there is nothing within.
My cup she never overfloweth
and 'tis I that moan and groaneth.
Some grey and white matter,
(Give me the Karma Mama
a jet to Mecca, Tibet or Jeddah.
To Salisbury; A monastery;
The longest journey; across the desert.
Across the weather; across the elements.
Across the water).

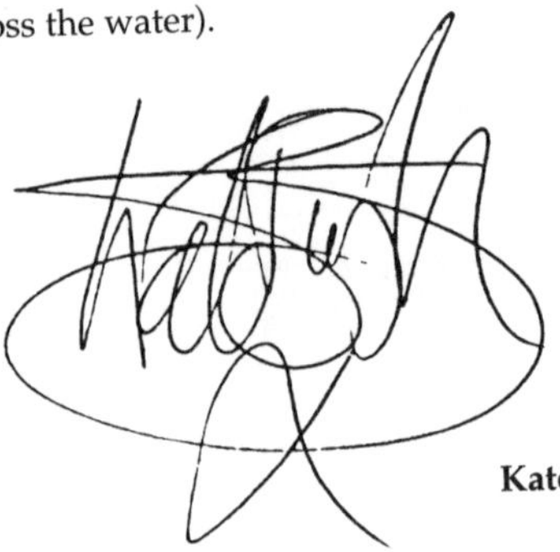

Kate Bush

MUSICIAN

...us, the poor, the needy and the notorious

Dear Father Michael,

Heaven is in itself eschatological reality. It is the advent of the finally and wholly Other. Its own definitiveness stems from the definitiveness of God's irrevocable and indivisible love. Its openness vis-à-vis the total eschaton derives from the open history of Christ's body, and therewith of all creation which is still under construction. Heaven will only be complete when all the members of the Lord's body are gathered in. Such completion on the part of the body of Christ includes the 'resurrection of the flesh.' It is called the 'Parousia' in as much as then the presence of Christ, so far only inaugurated among us, will reach its fullness and encompass all those who are to be saved and the whole cosmos with them.

And so heaven comes in two historical stages. The Lord's exaltation gives rise to the new unity of God with man, and hence to heaven. The perfecting of the Lord's body in the pleroma of the 'whole Christ' brings heaven to its true cosmic completion. The individual's salvation is whole and entire only when the salvation of the cosmos and all the elect has come to full fruition. For the redeemed are not simply adjacent to each other in heaven. Rather, in their being together as the one Christ, they *are* heaven. In that moment, the whole creation will become song. It will be a single act in which, forgetful of self, the individual will break through the limits of being into the whole, and the whole take up its dwelling in the individual. It will be joy in which all questioning is resolved and satisfied.

Joseph Cardinal Ratzinger

Cardinal Joseph Ratzinger. *Eschatology: Death and Eternal Life*
Prefect of The Congregation for the Doctrine of the Faith.
The congregation was created in 1542 by Pope Paul III
under its better – known title of the Holy Inquisition,
created to defend the Church from heresy.
Pope Paul VI gave the Congregation its present title in 1965.

Thoughts on heaven from the rich, the f

JOAN SUTHERLAND

Dear Father Michael,

I've had some 'curly' requests in my life but to be asked by you to provide 'words' on the subject of Heaven just about beats the lot!

Having been brought up in a church-going Presbyterian household, I have been sustained countless times by my faith in the Christian Church. 'Heaven' is something that has changed from a childhood idea of sitting about in the sky on fluffy clouds, sporting wings and singing praises to a harp and trumpet accompaniment to a haven from world turmoil and greed when our earthly life is over. I feel it is – a reward – a peace of mind for faithful stewardship.

Many thanks for your good wishes and congratulations on my retirement. The relief I am feeling at having shed the responsibility of 'delivering the goods' is somewhat 'Heavenly'!

With my very best wishes.

AC, DBE

Dame Joan Sutherland, AC, DBE, soprano, kindly wrote this letter shortly after her retirement concert at St. John's Smith Square, London.

us, the poor, the needy and the notorious

Thoughts on heaven from the rich, the p

Yehudi Menuhin

Dear Father Michael,

It all started with an invitation to a famous Catholic University which had asked me to talk to its students. Thus I started writing this prayer. Some time later I was asked to appear on a religious programme by the BBC. I wanted to reach people of all creeds, in all walks of life and, in particular, the young who are searching for ways of worship. I humbly hope that this, my prayer, will be of some value to those who seek.

To Thee whom I do not and cannot know – within me and beyond me – and to whom I am bound by love, fear and faith – to the One and to the Many – I address this prayer:

Guide me to my better self – help me make myself into one who is trusted by living things, creatures and plants, as well as the air, water, earth and light that sustain these, keep me as one who respects the mystery and the character of every variety of life in both its uniqueness and its mass, for all life is essential to its own survival.

Help me to preserve my capacity for wonder, ecstasy and discovery, allow me everywhere to awaken the sense of beauty, and with and for others and myself to contribute to the sum of beauty we behold, we hear, we smell, taste or touch or are otherwise aware of through mind and spirit: help me never to lose the life-giving exercise of protecting all that breaths and thirsts and hungers; all that suffers.

Help me to find a balance between the longer rewards and the shorter pleasures, while remaining in tune with relative values, while patiently according the passage of time its rich harvest of loyalties, experience, achievement, support and inspiration.

Help me be a good trustee for the body You gave me. No life is to do with as I will, not even my 'own', for it is like an object entrusted into 'my' temporary keeping, to bequeath back into the earthly cycle in the best possible condition for other life to continue.

Therefore, Thy will be done.

May those who survive me not mourn but continue to be as helpful, kind and

us, the poor, the needy and the notorious

wise to others as they were to me. Although I would love to enjoy some years yet, the fruits of my lucky and rich life, with my precious wife, family, music, friends, literature and many projects, in this world of diverse cultures and peoples I have already received such blessing, affection and protection as would satisfy a thousand lives.

Allow me to see and to feel and to try to ponder and to understand the relationship of the unity of the trinity in all its manifestations.

Help me in all confrontations to see the 'trialogue' as opposed to the 'dialogue'. Help me so that I may decide wisely on such apportionment of pleasure and pain as may fall within my jurisdiction.

And finally, whilst begging Thee to protect me from anger and condemnation, my own of others and others of mine, allow me unpunished to indulge in my particular aversions:

Enlighten them and me and help us to forgive each other.

Also with such enemies as I may possibly have, help me distinguish between the reconcilable and the irreconcilable, encourage me to seek by every means , understanding with the one whilst rendering the other ineffective, to learn from both and not deliberately to antagonise either.

Grant me the inspiration you have provided humanity, and encourage me to revere and to follow those living examples who enshrine your spirit – the spirit within and beyond each of us – the spirit of the One and the Many – the illumination of Christ, of Buddha, of Lao-Tsu and of the prophets, sages, philosophers, poets, writers, painters, sculptors, all creators and artists, and all the selfless people, the saints and the mothers, the known and unknown, the exalted and the humble, men, women – children of all times and all places – whose spirit and example remain with us and in us forever.

LORD MENUHIN, VIOLINIST

Thoughts on heaven from the rich, the

The **Mirror**

Arsenal are playing Tottenham Hotspur in the F.A. Cup Final. The score is 0-0 but Spurs have secured a controversial penalty in the 91st minute.

Teddy Sheringham, back at his old club on a free transfer from Manchester United and the Arsenal fans' most despised player ever, lines up against David Seaman.

He shoots, he scores - and starts one of the most gut-wrenching celebratory laps of honour ever seen on the hallowed turf.

Then it comes, the most magical beautiful sound I have ever heard. A whistle, quiet at first then building up to a piercing cacophony.

The referee has disallowed the goal, ordering a furious Sheringham to retake the kick.

He misses, and from the rebound Arsenal hoof the ball into the ether. Lurking in the ether is Dennis Bergkamp who looks up, spots the Spurs keeper Ian Walker standing outside his area - and shoots from the half-way line.

Walker sees the danger too late and desperately lunges backwards, his body twisting like a Florida hurricane. He claws the air, he clutches the air, the ball sails into the goal.

The whistle blows twice more, once for the goal, once more for full time.

Arsenal win 1-0, and Sheringham is sent off in the tunnel for dissent.

I have no idea what heaven is like. But if it is anything like that I can't wait to get there.

Piers Morgan, Editor of *The Mirror*

us. the poor, the needy and the notorious

House of Lords

Dear Fr. Seed:

Thank you for yr: letter of 24 Oct.

It is, I believe, impossible to write intelligibly ab.
heaven as such, and that for two reasons, each conclusive

The first is the limitation of human language of a
kinds to express the intense joy and ecstasy which admission t.
heaven will bring to the redeemed and saved as they ~~are~~
experience once and for all/to the beatific vision.

More deeply is that even when freed from the
constraints of language, our limited imagination cannot
even conceive the infinitude of beauty, love, and ~~other~~ activity
which presence in the heavenly court will bring.

Occasionally, in this life, one is vouchsafed a
pale reflexion of the reality, a faint echo of the heavenly truth.
One may catch a ~~clr~~ glimpse in the infinite trustfulness and
love in the face of a young child, the colour of a bird's plumage,

Thoughts on heaven from the rich, the

House of Lords

a glorious sunset or sunrise, a wide vista of mountain lakes peaks, snows, valleys, and lakes (It may be glimpsed in the song of a robin or a lark a bird, in a humanly made painting, poem, or melody. But these are only weak approximations to the real thing

The best thing I know about heaven is the utterly untranslatable hymn written by poor Peter Abelard in the first years of the twelfth century which begins:

"O quanta qualia sunt illa Sabbata
Quae semper celebrat suprema curia
Quae fessis requies), Quae merces fortibus,
Cum erit omnia deus in omnibus."

But each stanja, as it comes, Says something new & pierces the heart I wish I could do something better

yrs: sincerely,

Hailsham

Lord Hailsham
Former Lord Chancellor of Great Britain

137

House of Lords

Dear Fr. Seed,

It is, I believe, impossible to write intelligibly about heaven as such, and that for two reasons, each conclusive.

The first is the limitation of human language of all kinds to express the intense joy and ecstasy which admission to heaven will bring to the redeemed and saved as they experience once and for all time the beatific vision.

More deeply is that, even when freed from the constraints of language our limited imagination cannot even conceive the infinitude of beauty, love, and effortless activity which presence in the heavenly court will bring.

Occasionally, in this life, one is vouchsafed a pale reflection of the reality, a faint echo of the heavenly truth. One may catch a glimpse in the infinite trustfulness and love in the face of a young child, the colour of a bird's plumage, a glorious sunset or sunrise, a wide vista of mountain peaks, snows, valleys and lakes. It may be glimpsed in the song of a robin or a lark, in a humanly-made painting, poem, or melody. But these are only weak approximations to the real thing.

The best thing I know about heaven is the utterly untranslatable hymn written by poor Peter Abelard in the first years of the twelfth century which begins:

> O quanta qualia sunt illa sabbata
> Quae semper celebrat supema curia
> Quae fessis requies, quae merces fortibus,
> Cum erit omnia deus in omnibus.*

But each stanza, as it comes, says something new and pierces the heart.

I wish I could do something better for you.

Yours sincerely,

Hailsham

* O how great and how many are those Sabbaths
Which the heavenly court forever celebrates,
Rest for the weary, reward for the valiant,
When God will be all in all.

Thoughts on heaven from the rich, the

Heaven…

Death and Dying

Dear Michael,

Thanks so much for your letter. You set me a fearful challenge: but I cannot resist challenges - so here goes. If you confine it to the waste paper basket I shall not be in the slightest offended (or surprised!)

For me it has always been difficult to form a view on anything without hard facts. As regards heaven (or Nirvana) there are none available - merely generalised references by different religious leaders. I do believe (or at least have a strong hunch) that there is a continuation of life after death (what are we here for otherwise?) but my thoughts cannot take me any further and speculation serves no useful purpose: indeed it can cause apprehension and anxiety.

What I am convinced of is that the human brain is incapable of comprehending the mysteries of the universe. In so far as we *are* capable of applying logic to our eventual fate it must be that we shall be judged (or reincarnated) in accordance with our behaviour in this world towards our fellow human beings along the lines of how we have been brought up and taught. There is no logic in the suggestion that a devout Christian gets a better deal after death that a Hottentot who has conscientiously adhered to the rules of his tribe.

What is absolutely clear is that in forming any concept of afterlife spirituality must be kept apart from science: they simply do not mix.

Yours

Nicholas Eliott

For 30 years Nicholas Elliott was one of Britian's most successful spies and one of the most senior figures in MI6. He was known as one of the 'robber barons', and exposed Kim Philby in Beirut, in 1963.

Thoughts on heaven from the rich, the

Dear Michael,

Thanks so much for your letter. You set me a fearful challenge: but I cannot resist challenges — so here goes. If you confine it to the waste-paper basket I shall not be in the slightest offended (or surprised!). Sorry it has to be in m/s.

"For me it has always been difficult to form a view on anything without any hard facts. As regards heaven (or Nirvana) there are none available — merely generalised references by different religious leaders. I do believe (or at least have a strong hunch) that there is a continuation of life after death (what are we here for otherwise?) but my thoughts cannot take me any further and speculation serves no useful purpose: indeed it can cause apprehension and anxiety.

What I am convinced of is that the human brain is incapable of comprehending the mysteries of the universe. In so far as we are capable of applying logic to our eventual fate it must be that we shall be / judged (or reincarnated) in accordance with our behaviour in this world towards our fellow human beings along the lines of how we have been brought up and taught. There is no logic in the suggestion that a devout Christian gets a better deal after death than a Hottentot who has conscientiously adhered to the rules of his tribe

What is absolutely clear is that in forming any concept of afterlife spirituality must be kept apart from science: they simply do not mix."

Yrs

Nicholas

s, the poor, the needy and the notorious

ENOCH DUMBUTSHENA

Dear Father Michael,

When I was little my mind picture of heaven was a glorious one. It was clear and awesome. There was whiteness everywhere. There were no sinners so it seemed to me. There was no noise. Heaven was a holy place inhabited by good God-fearing people.

When I grew up a little I came to believe that my two grandmothers, who were Christians, and my maternal grandfather, a non-Christian, were in heaven. My grandfather was a gentleman and a caring man, and I could not imagine him out of heaven.

You may not think I had a paternal grandfather. I did. He was killed at the battle of the Shangani by Cecil Rhodes' settler army: he has no grave. I was born long after he was killed. Is he in heaven? I do not know. But he was fighting for justice.

I remember one day, I was cycling the eight miles between Makwiro Railway Station and Marshall Hartley Mission. It was dark. I was frightened. I thought that the spirits of my grandmother and my grandfather (non-Christian) and Jesus were accompanying me, moving with me but moving above tree tops. I cycled without fear until I arrived home.

You may want to know why I thought my grandfather was in heaven. My people the Shona and Ndebeles had a heaven where all good people went after death. The evil ones remained on earth haunting their relatives.

They had a God in heaven. He was reached through a line of good ancestors who would send one's prayers to him. But only the most venerable of them put the prayers to God. So we had a heaven before Christian missionaries came to Zimbabwe, and made the mistake of calling us pagans.

Although I am a Christian, I still hold the view that our ancestors, those who were good, are in heaven. I believe that when I depart from this earth I shall meet my grandparents in heaven and those of my Christian friends and relatives who have made it there. A heaven that is tranquil and serene is what I believe it is.

Enoch Dumbutshena
Former Chief Justice of Zimbabwe

Thoughts on heaven from the rich, the

An anonymous contribution

'Father,' he asked, 'will John go to heaven like you said at Mass?'

'Yes, I am sure that John is happy with God,' I replied.

The four homeless men were silent a while, thinking about John in heaven.

'But there's hell too.' another pointed out darkly.

The Catholic among the four remembered: 'There is a third place you can go. What's it called?...Pur...'

'Purgatory,' I interjected.

'Yes,' he said, 'a man can go to purgatory as well.'

'There are,' the first man summarised solemnly, 'three places you can be; heaven where you are with God, and purgatory where you suffer, And hell, that's here.'

'Here?' I enquired surprised. 'Is hell in this life?'

'Yes,' he said firmly. 'This life is hell.'

The other three agreed.

A conversation about a friend who died, between a Catholic priest and four homeless men in The Passage Day Shelter, London.

s. the poor, the needy and the notorious

ST. JAMES'S PALACE
LONDON S.W.1

Dear Father Michael.

I offer for reflection this passage from Canon Henry Scott Holland (1847-1918):

Death is nothing at all ... I have only slipped away into the next room ... I am I and you are you ... Call me by my old familiar name, speak to me in the easy way which you always used. Put no difference into your tone; wear no forced air of solemnity or sorrow. Laugh as we always laughed at the little jokes we enjoyed together. Play, smile, think of me, pray for me. Let my name be ever the household word that it always was. Let it be spoken without an effort, without the ghost of a shadow on it. Life means all that it ever meant. It is the same as it ever was. Why should I be out of mind because I am out of sight? I am but waiting for you. For an interval, somewhere very near just around the corner ... All is well.

Much love
Katharine

HRH The Duchess of Kent

Thoughts on heaven from the rich, the

…s, the poor, the needy and the notorious

FRANK MUIR

Dear Father Michael,

I can remind you of two quotations about heaven which I particularly enjoy, both treating heaven as a physical reality rather like the park with well-trimmed lawns and flower-beds which was the dog cemetery in Evelyn Waugh's *The Loved One.*

The first quotation, delightfully incomprehensible, came from Emmanuel Swedenborg (who was moved to found his sect, according to a contemporary, when an image of Jesus Christ appeared in front of him while he was enjoying a chop in a Ludgate Hill cookshop and said 'Eat slower'.) Swedenborg wrote: 'One of the wonders of heaven is that no one there is ever permitted to stand behind another and look at the back of his head.'

The second quotation came from the splendid old Countess of Cork and Orrery (1746-1840), blue-stocking, hostess and wit, who died at the age of ninety-four. As she was gently fading away, an old servant leant over the bed and murmured 'Take heart, my lady – in a moment or two you will be in heaven.' Milady opened an eye and said loudly, 'But I don't want to be in heaven – all that sitting about on damp clouds singing hymns!'

Frank Muir

THE LATE BROADCASTER, AUTHOR AND WIT

Thoughts on heaven from the rich, the

is, the poor, the needy and the notorious

Dear Father Michael

My favourite quote about heaven is by Martin Luther:

Be comforted little dog,
Thou too at the Resurrection
Shall have a little golden tail.

And the other lovely idea about heaven is that when you arrive, all your favourite dogs that have died come running across a wonderful green lawn to welcome you. Of course I would like my mother and father and my great friend Sophie and my Aunt Gwen and all the people that I have loved on earth that have died to be there too.

But I get so terribly upset about all the terrible cruelty to animals in the world that I would really like heaven to be particularly full of wonderful fields and lots and lots of delicious food, where animals can romp around having a lovely time and not eat each other, and dogs that had a terrible time on earth can find new wonderful angels to look after them.

It sounds so soppy, but I am so ashamed at what humanity has done to God's creatures that I would like Heaven to make some recompense, as to all the children that have been terribly abused and all the people that have been sad in life.

Sorry I have waffled on enough, this is a very woolly idea. I would also like it to be a wonderful party with lots of champagne and fun and celebrating the glory of God with all my friends.

Love,

Jilly Cooper

Writer

Thoughts on heaven from the rich, the

s, the poor, the needy and the notorious

Heaven...

And Peace

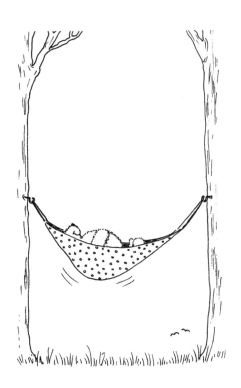

DENNIS SKINNER, M.P.

HOUSE OF COMMONS
LONDON SW1A 0AA

Dear Father Seed,

My idea of heaven on earth would be found in the countryside. An example would be a walk through Richmond Park enjoying the deer, squirrels, rabbits and birds. It would end up at Woodland Gardens, a section of the Park that is a true fantasy-land. Camelias and rhododendrons of exquisite and various colours dominate the scene. Magnificent magnolia trees of all ages abound as well. The many ancient tall trees form a shelter so that the garden becomes a beautiful sanctuary for anyone seeking peace and serenity - the objectives of heaven.

Best wishes

Yours sincerely

Dennis Skinner, MP

FORMER CHIARMAN OF THE LABOUR PARTY

Thoughts on heaven from the rich, the

...us, the poor, the needy and the notorious

DORA BRYAN, O.B.E., M.A.

Heaven is being on the beach or
in the garden on a sunny
day, with all my family.
Heaven will be the same
except all children will be
happy and there will be
PEACE.

ACTRESS

Thoughts on heaven from the rich, the

us, the poor, the needy and the notorious

JOHN LE CARRÉ

Penzance, Cornwall

Dear Father Michael **My Heaven**

I am very fond of the world I live in, and tend therefore to regard Heaven as an extension of it, rid of the things that annoy me. For example, Heaven will have no cars, roads, aeroplanes, helicopters or television. Rivers and seas will be pure, there will be no insecticides or plastic bottles, and simply masses of butterflies. Music will be celestial, nothing modern, and only for an hour or so in the evening, over the first whisky-and-soda. The climate will be cool but sunny, autumns will smell of woodsmoke, the landscape will be varied, very English and free of modern building.

Entry to Heaven is, of course, subject to my whim. Smith will be welcome. Smith was my Old English sheepdog. And he will have made up his quarrel with my two whippets, Mach II and Whisper, so they can be around too. No publishers or literary agents will be admitted. Any film agent daring to show his face at the gates had better look out. My children and grandchildren will be welcome, but to visit, not as residents. There will be no sectarian disputes, no Murdoch press or hairdressers who can't stop talking. Electrical equipment will have proper buttons to press or turn, and their instructions will be couched in plain English and printed in large lettering. And Forrest Spencer will apply in vain. I have never met Forrest, but today he wrote to me from Phoenix, Arizona to tell me, quite correctly, that I have repeated one particular phrase of English slang in practically every novel I have written. To be helpful, he gives me the page references. I'm sure Forrest is a good man in every way, but there are forms of literary perfection that have no place in Heaven, and his is one of them.

Best wishes
John le Carré

WRITER

Thoughts on heaven from the rich, the

s, the poor, the needy and the notorious

The **Oldie**

Dear Fr. Michael,
Here is a negative
view of heaven — the
best view I have
Kind regards
Richard Ingram

Heaven

No phones
No noise
No Traffic
No pain
No worries
No Telly
No papers
No flies
No sueues
No bores

R.I.

Richard Ingram, Editor of *The Oldie*.

Thoughts on heaven from the rich, the f

…s, the poor, the needy and the notorious

SIR R FLANAGAN, OBE, MA CHIEF CONSTABLE

For me, heaven will be a
place to appreciate everything
in child-like wonder. As
William Blake said,

"To see a world in a grain
of sand and a heaven in
a wild flower.
Hold infinity in the palm
of your hand and eternity
in an hour."

Ronnie Flanagan.

Ronnie Flanagan
Chief Constable, Royal Ulster Constabulary
Northern Ireland

Thoughts on heaven from the rich, the f

For me, heaven will be a
place to appreciate everything
in child-like wonder. As
William Blake said,
'To see a world in a grain
of sand and a heaven in
a wild flower.
Hold infinity in the palm
of your hand and eternity
in an hour'.

...us, the poor, the needy and the notorious

Thoughts on heaven from the rich, the

Michael Heath is cartoonist for *The Spectator*.

s, the poor, the needy and the notorious

Heaven…

Joy and Hope

Spike Milligan

Dear Father Michael,

I have a problem. I would like to believe in heaven and an afterlife but I can find no evidence of it. There is much spoken about the afterlife and the glories that it contains but personally I cannot feel that such a place exists; that does not stop me living a life of a good Christian whose philosophy, through the teaching of Jesus Christ, I try to observe closely mixed with a touch of Buddhism on the environmental side.

Shall I put it this way: I find heaven is on earth, I am stunned by the beauty of a blade of grass, can I say more.

If there is a heaven then I will consider it a bonus.

Love, light and peace,

Spike

SPIKE MILLIGAN.

COMEDIAN AND AUTHOR

Thoughts on heaven from the rich, the

...us, the poor, the needy and the notorious

Jeffrey Archer

House of Lords

Dear Michael,

I'm not altogether certain I shall make it myself, but I expect to be well ahead of some people I could name; nevertheless, I hope all my friends will get there, even though one or two have been rather naughty. I'm also rather hoping that God plays cricket, and if the rumour is true that God is an Englishman, then he can be the umpire.

With best wishes

Yours Sincerely

Jeffry Archer

AUTHOR

Thoughts on heaven from the rich, the

s. the poor, the needy and the notoricus

Thoughts on heaven from the rich, the p

PAUL GASCOIGNE
PROMOTIONS LTD

Dear Father Micheal
good luck With the Project

Day by day, day by day,
Oh, dear Lord, three things I pray
To see thee more clearly,
Love thee more dearly,
Follow thee more nearly,
Day by day,
Day by day
Day by day...

love
Paul
Gascoigne

Paul Gascoigne plays for the Everton football team. His favourite
prayer is based on that of St. Richard of Chichester, 1197-1253.

Thoughts on heaven from the rich, the f

...s, the poor, the needy and the notorious

FAIRWATER
SYDNEY, AUSTRALIA

Dear Father Michael,

Thank you for inviting me to give my views of 'Heaven'.

My first reaction is that it is a place of peace eternal, where people love one another.

Kindest regards
Mary Fairfax

Lady Fairfax, A.M., O.B.E.

LADY FAIRFAX, WIDOW OF SIR WARWICK, OWNER OF FAIRFAX NEWSPAPERS OF AUSTRALIA

Thoughts on heaven from the rich, the

THE DAILY MAIL LONDON

Telegrams, Daily Mail, London, W.8.

From: The Editor

Dear Father Michael,

Thank you for your letter and extremely kind invitation
to me to contribute to the new version of your book about
Heaven.

No one could fail to be moved by such an idea and I am
flattered by your interest in my contribution.

"My idea of Heaven is a beautiful garden in which I might
sit with my family, surrounded by flower beds that do not
need weeding, lawns that never require mowing, trees that
prune themselves, with the time to look and enjoy
everything around me."

I do hope this is the sort of thing you are after and
wish you all the best fortune with the book.

Yours sincerely,

PAUL DACRE   *Daily Mail (a division of Associated Newspapers Ltd)*

s, the poor, the needy and the notorious

NED SHERRIN

Dear Father Michael Seed,

I would have to take my cue from Sidney Smith but instead of foiegras & trumpets I would want caviare, oysters, pigs trotters, tripe and boudin noir to the sound of the voice of Elisabeth Welch.

Sincerely

Ned Sherrin

I would have to take my cue from Sidney Smith but instead of *foie gras* & trumpets I would want caviar, oysters, pigs trotters, tripe and *boudin noir* to the sound of the voice of Elisabeth Welch.

Sincerely

Ned Sherrin

BROADCASTER AND WRITER

Thoughts on heaven from the rich, the

s, the poor, the needy and the notorious

Trades Union Congress

Congress House, Great Russell Street, London WC1B 3LS

Dear Father Seed

Thank you for your letter– I enclose a small poem penned in
response, together with another on Heaven and Earth.
(I've always loved it.)

These are sent with some diffidence, unusual for the TUC.
After all, recent research has brought to light the TUC Prayer:

'Use us, O Lord,
Use thy servants – even if only in
an advisory capacity.'

Best wishes.

Yours sincerely,

Norman Willis

Former General Secretary

Thoughts on heaven from the rich, the

Trades Union Congress

Congress House, Great Russell Street, London WC1B 3LS

The Bells of Heaven

T'would ring the bells of Heaven
The wildest peal for years,
If Parson lost his senses
And people came to theirs
And he and they together
Knelt down with angry prayers
For tamed and shabby tigers
And dancing dogs and bears
And wretched, blind pit ponies
And little hunted hares.

Listed Value

Abu Ben Adhem (may his doubts increase!)
Awoke one morning, still bereft of peace,
Uncertain if the Angel's list was worth
As much in Heaven as it was on Earth.

after Leigh Hunt

s, the poor, the needy and the notorious

Heaven…

And Praise

The Rt. Hon. Ann Widdecombe, M.P.

Michael —
as Requested —
Heaven!

HOUSE OF COMMONS
LONDON, SW1A 0AA

'Go tell the Chief Whip, passers by, that here, alack, unpaired I lie' is probably the epitaph I shall choose for my gravestone with a passing apology to any Spartan I may meet in Heaven, although what a Spartan Heaven might be like beggars imagination.

Certainly Heaven has neither division bells nor whips with the possible exception of the Recording Angel who must quite often draw three ominous black lines under his jottings. I have long suspected him of setting up 'usual channels' with his earthly counterparts, for how else could they know so much about us?

Mine is in the traditional Christian Heaven – cherubim, white night-gowns, harps and sweet music (forced choruses and warbled hallelujahs says Milton's Satan rather unkindly, but presumably up there I shall warble in tune whereas down here I am tone deaf).

None of the other versions of Heaven bears contemplating. If I arrived in the underworld of the Ancient Greeks the first thing I would do would be to privatise the ferry service. The thought of standing on the bank while the Hades State Monopoly transferred my fellow-departed one by one would make London Transport very quickly look like Heaven. Anyway what could Charon do if I set up a fleet of privately operated profit-making ferries? He could hardly form a Union but come to think of it what could I do with the profits?

Then there was the Roman version which poor old Aeneas visited. No wonder he came back in a hurry. The trouble was that everywhere he went he kept meeting people he knew and they were not always pleased to see him. The more usual, if somewhat disconcerting, arrangement, whereby *they* visit *us* is much preferable.

Worse still would be Valhalla – endless battles interspersed with eating and drinking. I suppose I would not realise I had left the House of Commons but for the fact that the wounds would heal more quickly.

As John Wyndham once pointed out, the trouble with all these heavens is that they were designed by men for men. Women would have done it so much better. So night-gowns and harps, please and not a single divisional bell. I beg your pardon, St. Peter? Which door did you say I had to go through?

The Rt. Hon. Ann Widdecombe M.P.

Thoughts on heaven from the rich, the

...s, the poor, the needy and the notorious

PIERS PAUL READ

Dear Father Michael,

The images of paradise in the Koran and even the New Testament have always seemed to me more like purgatory than heaven. I can think of nothing more tedious than reclining on couches in gardens attended by dark-eyed houris; or attending an endless banquet in a dinner-jacket or a wedding reception in a morning-coat. On the other hand, I like dining with my friends; and the Church's teaching on the communion of saints promises the company of many men and women one has revered and admired. I feel almost impatient to meet St. Peter, St. Paul, St. Augustine, St. John Fisher, St. Thomas More, and many others. Heaven as I envisage it will be a reunion of old friends.

But the reunion with God will be much more than that, and here the image used by Jesus makes the mystery intelligible: that of resting in the bosom of Abraham. I loved my father and can remember how, as a child, I found a sublime refuge from all anguish and anxiety in his embrace. Heaven will not be a state of abstract ecstasy, but a final and eternal moment when all sorrows cease and all tears are wiped away.

Piers Paul Read.

AUTHOR

Thoughts on heaven from the rich, the

St James's Palace
London

Dear Father Michael,

Heaven to me is somewhat like infinity. It is impossible for us mere mortals to comprehend what it is like.

One morning not very long ago I was sitting with my wife by the sea – watching the sun come up over the horizon and listening to Fauré's Requiem. The beauty of it is difficult to describe – but if Heaven is anything like this – I for one will be more than content.

With kind regards.
Yours sincerely
Angus Ogilvy

The Rt. Hon Sir Angus Ogilvy KCVO

BUSINESSMAN

s, the poor, the needy and the notorious

John Dankworth

Dear Father Michael,

My idea of heaven is: Louis Armstrong, Bix Beiderbecke, Miles Davis, Dizzy Gillespie (trumpets), Tommy Dorsey, Jack Teagarden, Kid Ory, Frank Rosolino (trombones), Charlie Parker, Johnny Hodges, Lester Young, Stan Getz, Gerry Mulligan (saxes), Art Tatum (piano), Joe Pass (guitar), Charles Mingus (bass), Buddy Rich (drums), Duke Ellington (arranger/composer/leader), Count Basie (musical director) with Frank Sinatra, and Ella Fitzgerald (vocalists).

John Dankworth
Jazz band leader and composer

Thoughts on heaven from the rich, the

PREMIER
CHRISTIAN RADIO
1305 ● 1332 ● 1413 MW

Dear Father Michael,

I love the idea that when we take Holy Communion, we sort of "drop in" and join everyone in Heaven who are enjoying and eternal celebration of the Eucharist.

I also love the fact that I'm sure we'll all be very surprised when we see who is in Heaven – and as a broadcaster, I can't wait to have endlessly fascinating conversation with an amazing range of people!

Also, as a singer, I just know the music's gonna be great – and I can't wait to join in praising God!

Best wishes
Cindy Kent

Glen House
Stag Place ▪ London ▪ SW1E 5AG
Tel: **020 7316 1300** Fax: **020 7233 6706**
www.premier.org.uk email: premier@premier.org.uk

Premier is a trading name of London Christian Radio Ltd. registered in England Company No 2816074, which is wholly owned by the Christian Media Trust, registered charity No 287610

is, the poor, the needy and the notorious

From: The Rt. Hon. Alan Clark, M.P.

Dear Father Michael

*Here is my contribution to
your anthology:*

Heaven

Heaven is that place where all Nature lives in harmony. Where man, and animals, and birds and trees and crops and water all recognise in each other the gifts of God their creator. And where neither greed, nor cruelty, nor malice has any place, and the judgement of the Almighty is perpetual.

lots of love from us all —

The Rt. Hon. Alan Clark MP

Thoughts on heaven from the rich, the

...s, the poor, the needy and the notorious

Mark Reeve

Dear Father Michael,

My idea of Heaven!

REEVE: ..SO THIS FELLA SAYS.. URRRP.. .oop SCUZEME ,...
VOLTAIRE: MAGNIFICENT, A RATIONAL BELCH SIR!
LENNON: GREAT - .. FAB MAN.
WILDE: AN EPIGRAMMATIC ERUCTATION IF EVER THERE WAS ONE
SHAKESPEARE: WORTHY OF A PLAY — FORSOOTH
BYRON: OR AT LEAST A STANZA OR TWO.

Mark Reeve is a cartoonist for *The Express* newspaper
and has also worked on *Spitting Image*.

Thoughts on heaven from the rich, the

Heaven…

And Family & Friends

MELTON MOWBRAY
LEICESTERSHIRE

Dear Father Michael

An old American hymn used to tell us that 'anybody talkin'
'bout heaven ain't a-going there' and I am inclined to agree.
The possibility does become more interesting the older one
gets but for me heaven is the hope that remains after the
talking is done. Most people, I imagine, expect some sort of
immortality only through their offspring - and yet ... When the
question is put 'Is this all there is?' there is that residual doubt
which goes with a slow shake of the head. I like to hang on to
that doubt.

Yours truly

King

Lord King

FORMER HEAD OF BRITISH AIRWAYS

Thoughts on heaven from the rich, the

Julie Rogers

HERTFORDSHIRE

Dear Father Michael,

I suppose the first thing that comes to mind, having lost my dear Mum when I was seventeen, is to be reunited with her and, of course, all my loved ones in a world full of sunlight and flowers where disease and war are unknown. I certainly believe that the human spirit does go on in some form of energy and that there is a purpose to this life.

I should just like to add that in my ideal heaven, there should be plenty of shopping malls like Brent Cross, then I would really feel at home.

Ah well I can dream!

With love

SINGER

us. the poor, the needy and the notoriou.

SOHO PARISH SCHOOL
St. JAMES and ST. ANNE

Heaven is having the right coloured tops
on the felt-tip pens.
Vivien Hernandez

I think heaven is the best thing you could
imagine. Clean, lots of fountains, swimming
pools and everyone is well and everyone
are angels.
Ciara O'Sullivan

If you get hungry in Heaven God will give
you healthy food, like carrots.
Sajida Chowdry

Heaven is a peaceful place. I would think it
would be beautiful. Angels would be there.
You could sleep as long as you want.
Noah Cushing-Baker

Thoughts on heaven from the rich, the

SOHO PARISH SCHOOL
St. JAMES and ST. ANNE

In Heaven no-one hurts you or beats you up.
Christina Stones

I think that heaven is peaceful. No-one bullies anyone else, everyone is friendly and helps each other. Everyone sleeps on clouds and the underground train is gold, but no-one uses it because they got wings and can fly. Everyone lives in a cloud house, no-one is homeless or depressed, everyone is happy and never sad. God has a throne and you can go and visit him whenever you want. You go up a gold escalator and he is at the top.
Eve Farnese

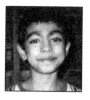

Heaven is a big magnet that sucks you up when you die.
Alim Sattar

I think heaven has lots of green meadows that never die. There is plenty of food and drink there, and there are houses for everyone. People are always well and never get ill. Everyone is always happy and love other people.
Isabelle Wright

us, the poor, the needy and the notoriou...

SOHO PARISH SCHOOL
St. JAMES and ST. ANNE

Heaven is a place where you can play games. It has food and drink. What I think heaven looks like is it's got things you could go to. God lives in heaven. I think there's money in heaven like a billion pounds or even more than that.
Fatima

Heaven is in the clouds with people with wings and playing instruments with baths and swimming pools all over the place where people can play all different sports without having to pay. Heaven is designed around what you like and enjoy. There are clouds all around the cemeteries (we can't see them) and we walk through them every time we visit a dead beloved one.
Sarah Holton

Thoughts on heaven from the rich, the p

wen PeePol goto
hevan tediY BeaPS
Keep you from
Beeing ShiBY SLeeping
in your Bed at
nite the first
nite you arive
Freddy MeconneL
age 6

When people go to heaven, teddy
bears keep you from being shy by
sleeping in your bed at night the first
night you arrive.
Freddy McConnel

us, the poor, the needy and the notorious

LESTER PIGGOTT
NEWMARKET

Dear Father Michael,

I hope that in Heaven I shall be able to meet up with The Chase; my first ever winner, and Palacegate Jack, my final one, as well as all those friends, both human and equine who have passed on during the intervening years. Like Denzil, I shall be hoping that those with whom I incurred some nasty injuries, have mended their ways!

Lester Piggott

JOCKEY AND RACE HORSE TRAINER

Thoughts on heaven from the rich, the f

FAREWELL LESTER

DEIGHAN

199

us. the poor, the needy and the notorious

Jeremy Paxman

Dear Michael,

I'd love to be able to help you with your book. But I lack the essential pre-requisite. My vicar says I'm fine on love, but get let down by hope, which is why I keep resisting my faith. I truly hope there is a heaven. But I can't imagine it.

With kind regard and best wishes for a happy and successful 1999

Jeremy Paxman

JOURNALIST AND TV PRESENTER

Thoughts on heaven from the rich, the

us, the poor, the needy and the notorious

Oifig an Taoisigh
Office of the Taoiseach

Dear Father Michael,

In Gaelic we have a lovely phrase *Ó Neamh go hÁrainn* which means 'anywhere' or 'all over the world', but literally it means 'from Heaven to Aran'.

To me Heaven is a place of stillness, tranquillity, contemplation, natural beauty and calm. At the same time some of mt happiest moments have been occasions of great tumult, noise, crowds, and tremendous hullabaloo.

I have found momentary heaven in great sporting moments for Dublin or for Ireland, and in moments of high political success, such as the signing of the Good Friday Agreement, or welcoming Archbishop Tutu and Nelson Mandela to Dublin, or succeeding in bringing some major high-Tech industry to Ireland.

But I have to say that the quiet moments with family, the gentle summer vacation evenings on a Kerry Beach, an autumn stroll in the Phoenix Park, or a helicopter flight over this breathtakingly beautiful country are the moments which have for me that spiritual dimension, which I believe is a foretaste of heaven.

I know that for many Irish exiles their native home is the heaven of their dreams, as that wonderful song Inisfree tells us, and their strong attachment and heart's longing is very akin to our spiritual longing for our true soul-home, because we know our hearts will never rest until they rest in the shadowland where all our family forebears, and all our national heroes await us.

Bertie Ahern

Bertie Ahern, Taoiseach (Prime Minister)of the Republic of Ireland

Oifig an Taoisigh, Tithe an Rialtais, Baile Atha Cliath 2.
Office of the Taoiseach, Government Building, Dublin 2.

Thoughts on heaven from the rich, the

us, the poor, the needy and the notorious

I BELIEVE IN **K**INGDOM **C**OME,
THEN ALL THE COLOURS WILL BLEED INTO ONE.

BONO OF **U**-2

LEAD SINGER OF ROCK BAND U2

Thoughts on heaven from the rich, the

...s. the poor. the needy and the notoricus

SIR CLIFF RICHARD

Dear Father Michael,
This seems apt.

For I have learned, in whatever state I am, to be content.
I know how to be abased, and I know how to abound;
in any and all circumstances I have learned the secret of facing
plenty and hunger, abundance and want.
I can do all things in him who strengthens me.
(Philippians 4:11-13)

Sir Cliff Richard OBE

SINGER

Thoughts on heaven from the rich, the

s, the poor, the needy and the notorious

THE SERMON ON THE MOUNT

Blessed are the poor in spirit,
  for theirs is the kingdom of heaven.
Blessed are those who mourn,
  for they shall be comforted.
Blessed are the meek,
  for they shall inherit the earth.
Blessed are those who hunger and thirst for righteousness,
  for they shall be satisfied.
Blessed are the merciful,
  for they shall obtain mercy.
Blessed are the pure in heart
  for they shall see God.
Blessed are the peacemakers,
  for they shall be called sons of God.
Blessed are those who are persecuted for righteousness' sake,
  for theirs is the kingdom of heaven.
Blessed are you when men revile you and persecute you,
  and utter all kinds of evil against you falsely on my account.
Rejoice and be glad,
  for your reward is great in heaven.

St Matthew's Gospel

Thoughts on heaven from the rich, the